Success
is a
Journey

Other Books by Jeffrey J. Mayer

*If You Haven't Got the Time to Do It Right,
When Will You Find the Time to Do It Over?*

Find the Job You've Always Wanted in Half the Time with Half the Effort

Winning the Fight Between You and Your Desk

Time Management for Dummies

Time Management for Dummies Briefcase Edition

ACT! for Windows for Dummies

ACT! 3 for Windows for Dummies

ACT! 4 for Windows for Dummies

Success
is a
Journey

7 Steps to Achieving Success in the Business of Life

Jeffrey J. Mayer

McGraw-Hill

New York   San Francisco   Washington, D.C.   Auckland   Bogotá
Caracas   Lisbon   London   Madrid   Mexico City   Milan
Montreal   New Delhi   San Juan   Singapore
Sydney   Tokyo   Toronto

Library of Congress Cataloging-in-Publication Data

Mayer, Jeffrey J.
    Success is a journey : 7 steps to achieving success in the
business of life / Jeffrey Mayer.
        p.   cm.
    Includes index.
    ISBN 0-07-041129-8
    1. Success in business.   2. Life skills.   I. Title.
HF5386.M472   1998
650.1—dc21   98-42939
                                                  CIP

McGraw-Hill

A Division of The **McGraw·Hill** Companies

1 2 3 4 5 6 7 8 9 0   DOC/DOC   9 0 3 2 1 0 9 8

ISBN 0-07-041129-8

Printed and bound by R. R. Donnelley & Sons Company.

To my wife Mitzi and my daughter DeLaine.
I love you both very much.

ACKNOWLEDGMENTS

There are many people who have contributed to the successful creation of this book, and I would like to thank and acknowledge them for their help and contributions.

I would like to begin by saying thank you to Betsy Brown, senior editor; Susan Barry, editorial director; and Philip Ruppel, vice president and publisher at McGraw-Hill. When I first pitched the idea for this book to Susan, I could tell by the tone of the telephone conversation that this was a book she was very interested in. Shortly thereafter Susan introduced me to Betsy, who told me that *Success is a Journey* was a book McGraw-Hill wanted to publish. Needless to say, I was thrilled.

It has taken more than a year to turn my manuscript into this book, and Betsy deserves a lot of credit for helping me to write such a great book. Betsy, it's been a pleasure working with you. I appreciate all of the help, assistance, and guidance you've given to me.

Kurt Nelson, Betsy's editorial assistant, is the glue that holds everything together. Kurt, thank you so much for getting answers to questions and responding to my queries so quickly.

Lynda Luppino is McGraw-Hill's marketing manager. Lynda, thank you for taking the time to work on the marketing and promotion of *Success is a Journey.*

I would like to thank art director Eileen Kramer and her staff for doing a great job designing *Success is a Journey*'s cover.

Elwood Smith is a very talented artist and one of the world's best illustrators. He's just brilliant. This is the third book Elwood has illustrated for me. I want to thank Elwood and Maggie Piccard, his wife and representative, for all their contributions to my literary works. You can see more of Elwood's work on his Web site, www.elwoodsmith.com.

McGraw-Hill put together an entire team of people to edit and design *Success is a Journey*. I would like to start by thanking Jane Palmieri, McGraw-Hill's editing supervisor. Jane did a masterful job of coordinating, scheduling, and overseeing the entire editorial process.

Jane assigned the task of editing and producing *Success is a Journey* to North Market Street Graphics in Lancaster, PA. Art Director Patti Kahler, Paginator Lisa Kochel, Customer Service Rep Ruthann Sherbine, and Copyeditor Stephanie S. Landis did just a wonderful job. I had many long conversations with Stephanie about the final editing of my book, and she was wonderful to work with. Thanks to all of you for all your help.

The final member of the editorial team was Beth Oberholtzer of Beth Oberholtzer Design in Lancaster, PA. Beth, thank you for doing a wonderful job of designing and laying out the pages of *Success is a Journey*.

I would like to say thank you to the people who are responsible for promoting *Success is a Journey*: Claudia Riemer-Boutote, director of publicity and marketing communications; Evan Boorstyn, associate director of publicity; and Lydia Rinaldi, senior publicist.

And finally, I would like to thank the two women in my life, my wife Mitzi and my daughter DeLaine, for their love, support, and encouragement during the two years it took me to research, write, and edit this book. They left me alone on the weekends so that I could write. And they didn't ask too many questions about why I was sitting at the computer at 4:00 A.M. on a Saturday or Sunday morning. I promise to make less noise in the future.

CONTENTS

Life and Work Have Become Hectic and Complicated   **1**

Where Are We Going with Our Lives?   2

What Is Success?   **3**

Success Depends upon Your Expectations   4

    What Were Your Expectations?   5

        How Did You Do on the Test?   5

        Did You Solve the Problem?   5

        Did You Close the Sale?   6

        Was the Company Successful?   7

        How Did the Team Do?   8

    Success Comes from Participation   11

    Some Things to Think About   12

The Thirteen Characteristics of Successful People   14

STEP 1

Successful People Have a Dream   **19**

Principle #1: Successful People Have a Dream   21

    Become a Dreamer   23

Principle #2: Successful People Have Fun   24

Principle #3: Successful People Have Desire   27

Principle #4: Successful People Have Faith   29

Principle #5: Successful People Make Their Own Luck   30

Principle #6: Successful People Aren't Afraid of Failure   33

    Overcome the Fear of Failure   35

Principle #7: Successful People Don't Quit!   36

Principle #8: Successful People Don't Take No for an Answer   38

What Have You Done with Your Life?   41
    What Have Been Your Major Accomplishments?   41
    What Are You Most Proud Of?   42
    What Are Your Skills and Talents?   43
    What Do You Value Most in Life?   45

STEP 2

Successful People Have a Master Plan of ACTion   47

Creating a Master Plan Saves You Time   49
    Put Your Plan on Paper   50
    Creating Your Master Plan   51
    Your Master Plan Is Constantly Changing   52
Create a Board of Directors to Help You Execute Your
    Master Plan   53
    Speak with Many Different People   55
        Listen to What Everybody Has to Say   55
        Get Rid of the Naysayers   56
    What Can You Do for Each Other?   56
What Do You Want?   57

STEP 3

Successful People Get Results   59

Clean Up the Clutter   61
    Cleaning Off Your Desk   61
        Tools of the Trade   62
        Cleaning Up the Mess in Four Easy Steps   63
    Organizing Your Desk Drawers   64
        Clean Out Your Desk File Drawer   65
    Setting Up Your Master File Drawer   66
        Setting Up Your Master Filing System   67
    Dealing with Reference Materials   69
        Setting Up a Reading File   70
        Read with a Pen in Your Hand   70
        Setting Up a Resources File   71
Using Your Master List   72
Put Your Master List Inside Your Computer   77
    You Need a Place to Store Personal Information   78

Activities Are Scheduled with People 81
View Your Tasks in Many Different Ways 82
    View Your Activities by Person 82
    View Your Activities as a List 84
    View Your Activities on a Calendar 85
The Power to Modify Activities 86
    Automatically Roll Over Your Unfinished Activities
      from One Day to Another 87
    Rescheduling Activities Is Easy 87
You Can Take It with You 88

STEP 4
Successful People Take Responsibility for Their Time   91

Increase the Value of Your Time 93
    Give Yourself a Raise 94
    Give Yourself an Extra Hour Each Day 96
    Do One More Thing Before You Call It a Day 97
Setting Your Priorities 99
    Successful People Don't Procrastinate 100
    Create a Sense of Urgency by Setting Deadlines 102
    Focus on the Important Tasks, Not the Urgent Ones 105
    Be the Person Who Solves Problems 107
    Take the Time to Solve Problems 108
Getting the Most out of Each Day 111
    Schedule an Appointment with Yourself 111
    Make the Most of Your Prime Time 113
    Give Yourself the First Two Hours of the Day 114
    Take Control of Your Meetings 116
    Avoid Impromptu Meetings 119
    Schedule Your Telephone Calls 120
    Schedule Time to Meet with Your Staff, Colleagues,
      and Co-workers 121
Taking Control of Your Day 123
    Technique #1: Identify Your Three Most Important Tasks 123
    Technique #2: Schedule Your Day 123
    Technique #3: Who Are Your Biggest Time-Wasters? 127
    Technique #4: Keep a Journal of Your Daily
      Accomplishments 127

STEP 5
Successful People Build Relationships with the *Right* People   129

Networking: The Art of Making Friends   131
Give Yourself the Opportunity to Meet a Lot of People   131
Networking with a Paper-Based System   134
  Obese Rolodex Files Aren't Usable   134
    Adding New People Is a Cumbersome Process   135
    Finding People Isn't Easy   136
    What Happens When a Person Changes Jobs?   136
  Name and Address Books Don't Work Either   137
  Business Card Files Just Collect Business Cards   137
Put Your Name and Address Book Inside Your Computer   139
  The Way I Used to Do It   139
  ACT! Is the Ultimate Networking Tool   140
    An Electronic Name and Address File   140
    It's Easy to Find People in ACT!   141
    Everybody's Got a Notepad   143
    ACT! Makes It Easy for You to Communicate
      with People   144
  Getting the Most out of ACT!   146

STEP 6
Successful People Get to Know the Important People in Their Lives   149

The Art of Networking   151
Get to Know the Friends of the Important People in Your Life   154
  Getting an Introduction   154
  The Art of Keeping in Touch   155
Networking Is a Lifelong Process   156
  Look for People with Whom You've Got Chemistry   156
Networking Within Your Own Organization   157
  Get to Know Your Boss Better   157
  Get to Know the Important People Within Your Company
    or Organization   158
  Get to Know the Important People Within Your Business
    or Industry   159
Who Are Your Most Profitable Customers?   160
  When You Have a Lot of Customers, You Have a Feeling
    of Security . . . False Security   160

Getting to Know People   163
  Basic Information   164
  Business or Professional Information   165
  Personal Information   165
  Outside Interests   166
  Goals, Dreams, and Desires   166
Spend Your Life Making Friends   166

STEP 7
Successful People Strive for Excellence   167

There Is No I in Team   169
  Asking For and Getting Help When You Need It   169
    The Art of Delegating   170
    Share the Limelight   171
Become a Brilliant Conversationalist   172
  The Art of Asking Questions   173
    Always Ask Open-Ended Questions   173
    Listen to Understand What the Other Person Is Saying   175
  The Art of Negotiating   179
    Know What You Want   179
    Look at the Situation from the Other Person's Point
      of View   180
  Make Everybody Feel Like a Winner   183
    Don't Get into an Argument   183
    But I'm Right . . .   184
    When You're Wrong   185
Make the Most out of Every Day   187
  Do Things ¼ of a Percent Better Each Day   187
  Set Daily Goals for Yourself   187
  Have a Great Day, Every Day   188
  Strive for Excellence   189
  Think Winning Thoughts   189
  Surround Yourself with Positive, Supportive People 190

Index   191

ABOUT THE AUTHOR

Photo: Roger Lewin

Jeffrey Mayer is one of the country's fore-most authorities on time and business management. For a living, he helps busy people get organized, save time, and become more productive. Jeff's claim to fame is his "clean desk" approach to time management.

USA Today dubbed Jeff "Mr. Neat, the Clutterbuster," and *People* called him "The Dean of the Desk Cleaners." *Esquire* stamped him: "The Productivity Guru."

He walks into an office that looks like a toxic waste dump—with piles of paper strewn all over the place—and in two hours the desktop looks like the flight deck of an aircraft carrier. So much is thrown away that the wastebasket is filled to the brim, overflowing, and spilling onto the floor. All that remains are a handful of file folders, a pad of paper, a computer, and a telephone. Everything else is neatly filed away.

Long ago, Jeff realized that if people were better organized, they could take more control over their day and would have more time to focus on their most important work. At the end of the work day, they could leave the office, go home, and spend more time with family and friends.

Jeff's clients realize that time is money, and Jeff is able to help them convert wasted time into time that can be used more efficiently, effectively, and profitably. Jeff's specialty is teaching people how to improve their follow-up systems. With a good follow-up system, a person is able to spend more time working on the things that are important, instead of the things that keep him or her busy.

Since the founding of his Chicago-based consulting firm, Mayer Enterprises, Jeff has helped tens of thousands of men and women (many are top executives at Fortune 500 companies) get organized, use their time more effectively, and make more money.

His corporate clients include American Express Financial Services, Commonwealth Edison, DDB/Needham Advertising, Encyclopaedia Britannica, LaSalle National Bank, Merrill Lynch, Navistar, Sears Roebuck & Co., and R. R. Donnelley & Sons Company, just to name a few.

Jeff has been interviewed by almost every major newspaper and magazine in the United States, including *The Wall Street Journal, The New York Times, Newsweek, People, Forbes, Business Week,* and *Fortune.* He has also been interviewed on hundreds of radio and television programs across the United States, including *The Today Show, American Journal,* CNN, CNBC, and *ABC News.*

Jeff also publishes a newsletter—ACT! in ACTion—for Symantec's ACT! contact management program. If you would like a free sample issue, complete the coupon at the back of this book or visit Jeff's Web site at www.ACTnews.com.

Jeffrey Mayer Would Like to Hear from You

Jeff would like to hear from you. How did you like this book? How did it help you find your life's calling? How can this book be improved? Please share your success stories with Jeff.

Jeff can be reached at:
Mayer Enterprises
50 East Bellevue Place, Suite 305
Chicago IL 60611

His phone and fax is (312) 944-4184.
His e-mail address is jeff@ACTnews.com.
You can visit his Web site at www.ACTnews.com.

Jeffrey Mayer Would Be Delighted to Speak at Your Next Business Meeting, Conference, or Convention

Jeff would be delighted to speak at your next business meeting, conference, or convention. For date availability, he can be reached at the addresses mentioned previously.

Success
is a
Journey

Life and Work Have Become Hectic and Complicated

Life and work have become hectic and complicated. There's too much to do and not enough time. We rush from one meeting to another to another to another. And when we return to the office there are five, ten, fifteen, twenty, or more voice mail messages that need to be returned, and scores of e-mail messages to reply to—and we've only been gone for a few hours.

On our desks are piles of papers that we've got to do something with. There are letters to write, proposals to prepare, things to follow up on, and lots of other miscellaneous *stuff* that's been hanging around for days, weeks, or months.

On the computer monitor we've attached yellow, blue, and green sticky notes as reminders of things to-do or people to call. Our in- and out-boxes have become hold boxes filled with unopened mail, faxes, express delivery letters, and who knows what else. And we spend most of our days putting out one fire after another.

When we leave the office we take our laptop computer—so we can check our e-mail and search the Internet—our mobile phone, and our beeper. We're afraid to be out of touch for even a few moments.

In order to *try* to stay on top of things we come in early, stay late, work weekends—and never seem to catch up.

Where Are We Going with Our Lives?

Something's getting lost in all of this chaos and mayhem. We're so busy, and working so hard, that we've lost track of what we *really* want to be doing with our lives. What we *really* want to do for ourselves. What we *really* want to do for our families.

Yes, we've got a job. Yes, we're making a living and paying the bills. But we've forgotten the goals, dreams, and desires of our youth. We're putting in a lot of hard work and effort, but it isn't giving us the inner feelings of satisfaction and fulfillment we need or the success we once dreamed of achieving. We're so busy we don't have time to think about, let alone answer, the age-old question: "What do I want to do when I grow up?"

Success is a Journey will show you how to make your dreams come true. It will give you the tools you need so you can discover what you were born to do. It will help you develop a Master Plan of ACTion and then implement that plan. And, most importantly, it will get you to start thinking about who you are, what means the most to you, and what you want to do with your life.

What Is Success?

For years I have been fascinated with the subject of success. How do you define it? What does it mean? Is it temporary? Is it permanent?

As I've pondered these questions in my mind and watched the performance of others, I have come to the realization that success is not an end result. It is an ongoing process. It's a journey.

However, there's an ebb and flow to success. It's not linear. It comes and goes. There are ups and downs. One day you have a great day, the next day is so-so, and the third is absolutely rotten. But on the fourth day, something good happens, and you're back on top of the world again. Or you may have a great morning and a rotten afternoon, or vice versa. Or, maybe you have a bad year or season, but the next one is much better. That's life!

REMEMBER

Successful people never quit. When they suffer a setback, they just pick themselves up and keep going.

To be successful in the business of life you build upon your successes. You set goals—achievable goals—for yourself, and accomplish them. Then you set slightly more difficult goals, and go out and accomplish them.

SUCCESS TIP

Follow this process over and over throughout your life and you'll accomplish more than you ever dreamed.

The ultimate goal in life isn't just to succeed, it's to continue to succeed. To continue to improve. To continue to be the best that you can be. The best in your business, profession, or chosen career. The best husband, wife, father, mother, son, daughter, and friend. You only have one life, and you have the opportunity to make it a great one. The future is yours, and it's unlimited. You can make it into anything you want.

Success Depends upon Your Expectations

Life isn't lived in a vacuum, and whether or not any of us is successful in any endeavor is determined by our expectations before we started. We've got to know the criteria on which we're going to judge ourselves or be judged by others. Most of us are never 100 percent successful in any of the things that we do. But the goal is to try our best, learn from our experiences, and take the knowledge we gain along with us so we can do the task even better the next time.

SUCCESS TIP

Write your goals and objectives on paper before you embark upon any task. This enables you to compare your results or accomplishments with your expectations.

What Were Your Expectations?

I find the whole subject of whether or not a person is successful to be very complex. It's usually not black or white. The results are very dependent upon a person's long- and short-term expectations—in addition to his or her skills, talents, and training and a host of other factors that may or may not be within the person's control.

Here are some examples of how difficult it can be to try to determine a person's degree of success.

How Did You Do on the Test?

When you were going to school I'm sure you had to take lots of tests. (I know I sure did.) Did you ever spend a lot of time studying and preparing for a test, yet not do as well as you had hoped? How did you feel? Disappointed, I'll bet.

On the other hand, how did you feel when you did very well on a test that you hadn't spent much time studying for? Lucky?

What were your feelings when you got the grade that was representative of the work and effort you put into your studies? For myself, deep down inside I always knew I had gotten what I deserved.

And what happened when you showed your parents your report card? Did it measure up to their expectations?

You see, success depends upon your expectations.

ANECDOTE

I had a friend who studied every day and went through four years of college and *may* have gotten a single B. He got an A in every other class he took. His expectations were so high that if he had gotten anything less than an A, in his mind he would have failed. I didn't have the same expectations or work ethic. I was pleased when I got a B and was on cloud nine when I got my occasional—very occasional—A.

Did You Solve the Problem?

Every day you've got problems to solve. Things need to be done for your boss or supervisor, customers call with problems or questions, and you've got lots of tasks that need to be completed. You probably haven't looked at it this way, but you should consider yourself successful when you solve the problem, answer the question, complete the task, and get the work done.

Now the completion of these tasks may not be what you would consider to be a big success, but it's one more thing you've learned that you can take with you on your journey through life. And it's one more thing you can cross off your list of things to-do.

But what if you work very hard to accomplish a specific task and aren't 100 percent successful in completing the endeavor?

Or what if it took longer than expected?

Or what if you found that you weren't able to solve the problem (but learned something new because of the experience)?

Are you a success or a failure?

Did You Close the Sale?

If you're in sales, you may feel that you're a success when you close a really big sale. But when you were just getting started in your career, you probably felt like you were on cloud nine when you closed your *first* sale, no matter what the size. And if you're a seasoned pro, but you've been in a slump, that next sale may make you feel like you're on top of the world.

Let's take another example. A salesperson leads her company in sales one year, but doesn't do it the next. What if she did in fact sell more the second year, but was still outsold by someone else? What if she closed more sales, but made less money? Or closed fewer sales, but made more money?

Did she have a successful year? Was she a success or a failure?

ANECDOTE

One day a young man was making a life insurance presentation. After a long period of discussion, the prospect finally said, "I'll buy it." As the salesman was completing the forms the new customer started telling the young man how he should have conducted the sale. After a few moments, the young man looked up and said: "I made the sale, didn't I?"

Was the Company Successful?

How do you determine whether a company is successful? That depends once again upon your position and your expectations. For example, the board of directors of a corporation may look at whether or not management is successful and doing a good job from the perspective of how much money the company made from one quarter or fiscal year to the next.

However, if the company is a public corporation, the board, its stockholders, and the analysts that follow the stock may look at the value of the company's stock, its earnings per share, or its earnings as compared to those of its competitors as an indicator of whether or not it has been successful. And though each group of people is looking at the same financial information, each will probably come up with different conclusions and opinions.

If, on the other hand, the company is a small start-up and is brand new, success may be determined by whether or not there's enough cash to pay the bills at the end of the month.

ANECDOTE

There's a scene in the James Stewart classic *It's a Wonderful Life* where there is a run on the family bank. George Bailey, played by Mr. Stewart, is ecstatic when the bank is able to close its doors at 6:00 P.M. and still has two dollars—yes, TWO DOLLARS—left. They've made it through the day and are still in business.

The expectations of an established company may be quarter-to-quarter, or year-to-year, while for the new company, success may be measured on a day-to-day or week-to-week basis.

THE STOCK MARKET PASSES ITS OWN JUDGMENT

Publicly traded companies are judged by investors and stock market analysts in addition to their stockholders and their boards of directors. Sometimes they judge success in strange ways. Bizarre as it may seem, many companies' stock prices have gone up because everybody expected them to lose a lot of money, and they lost less than expected. And the stock prices of other companies have fallen because they didn't make as much money as was anticipated.

Here are some examples of how the stock market passes its own judgment as to who is and isn't successful:

- The Oracle Corporation raised the earnings caution flag, and its shares lost 29 percent of its market value—$9.44 billion—in one day. Lawrence J. Ellison, the company's chairman, suffered a paper loss of about $2 billion.

- The Plexus Corporation, an electronics company, announced that its earnings would fall short of expectations because customers were delaying orders. Its shares fell 44 percent, from $25 to $14, in one day.

- Silicon Graphics shares went up 22 percent in one day when it was announced that Richard E. Belluzzo, the number two man at Hewlett-Packard, had agreed to become chairman and chief executive of the troubled computer company. Analysts and Silicon Graphics customers felt Belluzo was a higher-level executive than they had expected the company to attract.

How Did the Team Do?

In sports, a team that wins a championship is considered to be a success. But what about the runner-up? Were the members of that team *really* losers? Once again it depends upon expectations. If the runner-up was expected to win the whole thing, then maybe that team had a bad year. But what if they were picked to finish dead last, made it to the finals, and then lost? Were they losers or did they have a great year because they got to the championship?

And what if the star on the championship team played poorly and didn't contribute at the level that was expected of him? Does he feel like a success? What if the star of the losing team had a great series, but the team still lost?

And what about the person who has an MVP year, but never performs at that level again?

ANECDOTE

I remember reading about a runner who finished second in one of the sprint races at a recent Olympics. He was disappointed that he didn't win, but he had still run faster than he ever had before. He just wasn't fast enough to win the race that afternoon. He couldn't decide if he was a winner or a loser.

WHO WON, WHO LOST?

In the fall of 1997, *HomeCourt,* the official magazine of the Utah Jazz, created a special commemorative issue entitled "The Finals." This was a special keepsake magazine celebrating the team's participation in the NBA championship series. Each game of the finals was recounted with loving words and photographs.

In Chicago things were different. The Chicago Bulls' management was treating coach Phil Jackson with disdain. They made it clear they weren't sure they wanted him back as the team's head coach. They let it be known that Bulls star Scottie Pippen would probably be traded. And Michael Jordan stated that he wouldn't play for another coach if Phil Jackson wasn't rehired. The entire city was having a panic attack.

You would have thought that the Jazz had won and the Bulls had lost. Right? Wrong! The Bulls won the championship, had just won back-to-back titles, and had been champions for five of the last seven years. Yet management was telling the fans that all good things must come to an end.

In the end, Phil, Scottie, and Michael stayed (they beat the Utah Jazz in the 1998 NBA finals to win their sixth championship in eight years), but you would never have known it by watching the way each team reacted after the conclusion of the 1997 NBA championships.

So how do you look at success? You have two criteria:

1. You have to look at success within certain time frames: moment-to-moment, day-to-day, month-to-month, year-to-year, or over an entire lifetime.

2. You have to consider what your expectations were before you started.

DID TIGER HAVE A GOOD YEAR?

For most golfers, any of these achievements would constitute a good year: winning the Masters by a record-setting 12 strokes. Winning more tournaments (four) than any other player on the tour. Becoming the first golfer on the tour to win more than $2 million in a single season.

Tiger Woods did all of the above in the first half of his first full season on tour, at the ripe old age of 22. But Tiger didn't perform very well during the second half of the 1997 tour. He played in eight tournaments, had no victories and only two top 10 finishes, and earned just $300,000 of his year's total of $2,066,833.

Tiger Woods lives in a world that is different from yours and mine. He is expected to win every tournament he enters. And when he doesn't it's big news. So let me ask you: Was Tiger a success or a failure?

IS A 9-7 FOOTBALL TEAM THAT DOESN'T MAKE THE NFL PLAYOFFS A SUCCESS?

The New York Jets had the worst record in professional football during the 1996 season, when they went 1 and 15. Then Bill Parcells became their head coach. He changed players. He changed habits. He changed attitudes. And the team started to win.

The Jets could have clinched a playoff berth with a victory in the last game of the season. But they lost to Detroit 13-10 on a day when super running back Barry Sanders rushed for his 2000th yard of the season. Did the Jets have a successful season?

Success Comes from Participation

You see, everything in life depends upon your frame of reference: where you are, where you came from, and where you want to go.

 REMEMBER

You should feel that you are a success when you try, when you participate, when you go out there and put your butt on the line.

Success is the act of trying to improve upon the things you're already doing. It's growing and developing. It's accepting bigger and greater challenges. It's not being afraid of making a mistake, suffering a setback, or failing. It's trying to do your very best.

And if, in the end, your very best wasn't quite good enough, you just have to go back to work and prepare a bit harder for the next time.

It is through the act of participating, as you try to achieve your goals, that you succeed. Nobody succeeds 100 percent in anything they do. When you're able to recognize and accept this fact of life, you realize that failure and losing are as much a part of the game of life as are success and winning.

So embrace your goals, dreams, and desires. Pour your energy into completing those daily tasks. Go out and play your game, and play it to win! But don't think *only* of winning games, think of winning championships!

Some Things to Think About

Now I would like you to take a few moments to think about some of the things that have happened in your life. If you would like to write your thoughts down on the pages of this book, I've included some blank lines for you to do so. Or you can use a pad of paper or your word processor.

Think about all the things you've done in the past year. What are three things you did that greatly exceeded your expectations?

1. _____

2. _____

3. _____

Why did these accomplishments exceed your expectations? How did that make you feel?

_____

_____

_____

What are three things you've done in the recent past that failed to meet your expectations?

1. _____

2. _____

3. _____

What could you have done differently?

_____

_____

_____

What did you learn from these experiences?

_____

_____

_____

_____

What were the long-term ramifications?

_____

_____

_____

One more thing to think about: Were your expectations realistic?

The Thirteen Characteristics of Successful People

I've spent many years studying successful people and have identified the skills, talents, and characteristics that enable them to succeed. As you look at and study these skills, talents, and characteristics, you'll realize that you possess many of them yourself. Some of these skills and talents are more dominant than others and will play a greater part in your being, or becoming, a success in the business of life. These are the things you do well. The things you do easily and effortlessly. These are your strengths.

When you find you need a skill or talent you don't have, just go out and look for a person or group of people with the skills, talents, and training you need. Skills and talents that complement your own. These people will become your teammates, colleagues, co-workers, professional advisors, and friends. With these combined skills and talents organizations grow, prosper, and become successful.

These are the five things you'll find every successful person has in common:

1. They have a dream.

2. They have a plan.

3. They have specific knowledge or training.

4. They're willing to work hard.

5. They don't take no for an answer.

 REMEMBER

Success begins with a state of mind. You must believe you'll be successful in order to become a success.

The following is a list of the skills, talents, and characteristics you'll find in successful people:

1. **Successful People Have a Dream.** They have a well-defined purpose. They have a definite goal. They know what they want. They aren't easily influenced by the thoughts and opinions of

others. They have willpower. They have ideas. Their strong desire brings strong results. They go out and do things that others say can't be done.

REMEMBER

- It only takes one sound idea to achieve success.

- People who excel in life are those who produce results, not excuses. Anybody can come up with excuses and explanations for why he hasn't made it. Those who want to succeed badly enough don't make excuses.

2. **Successful People Have Ambition.** They want to accomplish something. They have enthusiasm, commitment, and pride. They have self-discipline. They're willing to work hard and to go the extra mile. They have a burning desire to succeed. They're willing to do whatever it takes to get the job done.

REMEMBER

With hard work come results. The joy in life comes with working for and achieving something.

3. **Successful People Are Strongly Motivated Toward Achievement.** They take great satisfaction in accomplishing a task.

4. **Successful People Are Focused.** They concentrate on their main goals and objectives. They don't get sidetracked. They don't procrastinate. They work on the projects that are important, and don't allow those projects to sit until the last minute. They're productive, not just busy.

5. **Successful People Learn How to Get Things Done.** They use their skills, talents, energies, and knowledge to the fullest extent possible. They do the things that need to be done, not just the things they like to do. They are willing to work hard and to commit themselves to getting the job done.

REMEMBER

Happiness is found in doing and accomplishing, not in owning and possessing.

ANECDOTE

Many years ago I was asked the question: "Jeff, do you like pleasing habits or pleasing results?" As I pondered that probing question, and squirmed in my chair like a worm at the end of a hook, I felt as if I had painted myself into a corner. A few moments later I answered: "I like pleasing results." From that moment on my life changed. I began to do the things that were difficult, because that would enable me to achieve my goals.

6. **Successful People Take Responsibility for Their Actions.** They don't make excuses. They don't blame others. They don't whine and complain.

7. **Successful People Look for Solutions to Problems.** They're opportunity-minded. When they see opportunities they take advantage of them.

8. **Successful People Make Decisions.** They think about the issues and relevant facts, give them adequate deliberation and consideration, and make a decision. Decisions aren't put off or delayed, they're made now!

SUCCESS TIPS

- Spend more time thinking and planning before you make your decision, and you'll make better decisions.

- When you don't get the expected results from the decision you've made, change your course of action. Decisions should never be carved in stone.

9. **Successful People Have the Courage to Admit They've Made a Mistake.** When you make a mistake, admit it, fix it, and move

on. Don't waste a lot of time, energy, money, and/or other resources trying to defend a mistake or a bad decision.

REMEMBER

When people are wrong, they may admit it to themselves. If they are handled gently and tactfully, they may admit it to others and even take pride in their frankness and broad-mindedness. But people become very defensive and angry when others try to cram their mistakes down their throats.

10. **Successful People Are Self-Reliant.** They have the skills, talents, and training that are needed in order to be successful.

11. **Successful People Have Specific Knowledge, Training, and/or Skills and Talents.** They know the things they need to know to be successful. And when they need information, knowledge, or skills and talents that they don't possess, they find someone who does possess them.

12. **Successful People Work with and Cooperate with Other People.** They have positive, outgoing personalities. They surround themselves with people who offer them help, support, and encouragement. They are leaders.

13. **Successful People Are Enthusiastic.** They're excited by what they're doing, and that excitement is contagious. They draw people to them because these people want to work with them, do business with them, and be with them.

STEP 1

Successful People Have a Dream

There are eight principles of success that every successful person follows. Make these principles your own and you'll do more with your life than you ever dreamed.

Principle #1: Successful People Have a Dream

To be successful you've got to have a dream, a vision, a burning passion, a magnificent obsession. You've got to want something, and you've got to want it bad. This dream/goal/obsession has to become your prime motivator.

It takes enthusiasm, commitment, pride, a willingness to work hard, a willingness to go the extra mile, a willingness to do whatever has to be done in order to get the job done. To get the things you want in life you need motivation, drive, and energy.

 ANECDOTE

Keith Reinhard, the chairman and CEO of DDB Needham, was obsessed with a single goal: to win back the McDonald's advertising account he had lost in 1981. Over the next 15 years Reinhard showered McDonald's with unsolicited ad campaigns. He traveled around the world to land morsels of McDonald's overseas advertising business. He even peppered his conversations with quotes from McDonald's founder Ray Kroc. He kept in touch with the McDonald's marketing people, and in 1991 began to meet regularly with Paul Schrage, the company's chief marketing officer. Five years later McDonald's began to rethink its advertising strategy and ultimately awarded the business to DDB Needham.

THE RETURN OF JOHN GLENN

On February 20, 1962, John Glenn orbited Earth three times aboard his Mercury capsule, *Friendship 7,* and became a national hero. But he always felt frustrated because he never had the opportunity to get back into space. In 1996 he proposed to Daniel S. Goldin, NASA's administrator, that he be allowed to return to space as a "guinea pig" to show that space research might benefit the elderly. Glenn discussed this idea with NASA officials about 50 times over the next two years. In January 1998, NASA announced that Glenn, at the age of 76, would be allowed to journey again into space and "show that senior citizens have the right stuff."

The deeper your passion, the deeper your commitment, the greater the likelihood you'll become the success you dream of becoming. And when you have this deep passion and commitment, you're no longer working. You no longer have a job. You're doing something you love, and surprisingly someone's willing to pay you to do it. You're having fun.

SUCCESS TIP

Fix firmly in your mind what it is you want to do; then go out and do it!

The challenge comes in finding the thing in life that is your burning passion, your burning desire. So let me ask you:

● What is your burning passion?

● What is your burning desire?

● What do you dream of doing?

● What do you dream of accomplishing?

● What were you born to do?

I WAS BORN TO:

_____

_____

_____

_____

_____

If you don't yet know what your burning passion is, it's OK. Don't give it a second thought. Just keep reading, thinking, and dreaming. Throughout this book I'll be giving you more tools you can use to discover what you were born to do. Don't be in a hurry: It's unlikely you'll make this discovery overnight. And once you do, it may take several years, or even a lifetime, for you to fulfill your dream. That's the thrill of life.

REMEMBER

It is the search to discover what you were born to do that makes living so meaningful, interesting, and challenging.

ANECDOTES

● Some people reach their peak when others would consider them way beyond their prime. Here are two examples:

> Winston Churchill was 66 years old in the spring of 1940 when he became Great Britain's wartime prime minister. His political career was presumed to have ended in January 1932.

> Ray Kroc was 55 years old when he purchased the McDonald brothers' small chain of hamburger stands. He turned the chain into the McDonald's Corporation.

● Fanny Blankers-Koen attended the 1936 Olympic Games as an 18-year-old track and field competitor. She was so inspired by Jesse Owens' performance that she vowed to win a medal for the Netherlands in 1940. But the 1940 and 1944 games were canceled due to World War II. By the time the 1948 London games rolled around, Blankers-Koen was 30 years old and married with two children. She figured her best days were past, but competed anyway. She won four gold medals.

Become a Dreamer

Become a dreamer. Dream about the things you want to do. The things you want to accomplish. The things you want to have. The bigger your dreams, the bigger your successes.

REMEMBER

First, you've got to dream it. Then you've got to work your butt off to make your dream come true.

Share your dreams with your friends, your family, your co-workers, and your colleagues. Find people who want to become your teammates. Search for people who can provide you with support, advice, and encouragement. People who will help you turn your dream into reality. People who are as excited about your dreams as you are.

SUCCESS TIPS

- **Get rid of the naysayers. You can't allow yourself to be surrounded by people who aren't supportive and enthusiastic. These people will do nothing but pull you down, sap you of your energy and enthusiasm, and force you to spend lots of time convincing them that you *can* do the things you dream of doing.**

- **Strive for excellence and greatness in everything you do.**

In order to make your dream come true you must first create a plan of action—a Master Plan—and then you must execute the plan. (This is discussed in Step 2.)

Who are five people who will support you as you strive to make your dream come true?

1. _____

2. _____

3. _____

4. _____

5. _____

Make it a point to speak with these people regularly. Keep them abreast of everything that's going on in your life.

Principle #2: Successful People Have Fun

Whatever you do in life, you've got to have fun doing it. You've got to enjoy what you're doing. You've got to enjoy spending time with the people with whom you're working. You've got to like the people who are your customers and/or suppliers. The people with whom you interact every day.

If for some reason you aren't having fun, you aren't happy, you aren't achieving the pleasure, satisfaction, and/or enjoyment you feel you should have, then it's time to start planning your next career move.

That's what I find great about life. Everything's done by the process of elimination. Give yourself the opportunity to do, try, and experience many different things. Discover the things you *don't* like to do, and then try something else.

When things feel good, and you're getting whatever it is you need and want, then you should stay put. When strains, pressures, and/or tensions begin to develop, these are the warning signals that something's wrong. If they persist, then maybe it's time to make a change.

REMEMBER

It's not a disaster to take a job and discover that you don't like it. It only becomes a disaster when you choose to stay.

SUCCESS TIP

When you don't enjoy your work, or the environment in which you're working, it's impossible to be successful.

TWO POWERFUL THOUGHTS

Always keep these two powerful thoughts in mind:

● Make your work play, and your play work.

● Find a job you love to do, and you'll never work another day in your life.

Think for a few moments about what you just read. Read these thoughts a second and a third time. These are simple, but very important, concepts.

People rarely succeed at anything unless they have fun doing it. You must receive a feeling of satisfaction from your work. It must be rewarding for you. If it's not, all you've got is a job you must go to every day.

REMEMBER

When you love something it has value to you. When something is of value you spend time doing it, you spend time enjoying it, and you take care of it.

TAKE ME OUT TO THE BALL GAME

Harry Caray grew up with a passion for baseball and a desire to be a broadcaster. He got his first job as an announcer with the St. Louis Cardinals in 1945, and spent the next 54 years broadcasting games for the Cardinals, the Chicago White Sox, and the Chicago Cubs. Caray made dull teams sound exciting and urged fans to come out to the *old*—never *new*—ball park. He loved baseball with all the trimmings. Throw the ball. Hit the ball. Catch the ball. Have a Bud.

During the seventh-inning stretch Harry always sang "Take Me Out to the Ball Game." Then one day Bill Veeck, the owner of the White Sox, noticed that the fans right below the booth were listening to Harry through the flooring and singing along. For years, Veeck had been waiting for the right guy to sing "Take Me Out to the Ball Game." The next night, Veeck decided to hide a public address microphone in the booth. When the organist began playing "Take Me Out to the Ball Game," Harry began singing and Veeck threw the switch. All of a sudden Harry heard about 10,000 voices booming back at him. Veeck had correctly predicted that once you heard Harry sing you would join in because you knew you could sing better than him, and a tradition was born. In 1989 Harry Caray was awarded entry into the broadcasters' wing of the Baseball Hall of Fame. He said: "I always tried, in each and every broadcast, to serve the fans to the best of my ability. In my mind, they are the unsung heroes of our great game."

He loved life. He loved people. He loved baseball. There was nothing in the world he enjoyed more.

What are five things that you love to do so much that you would do them for free?

1. _____

2. _____

3. _____

4. _____

5. _____

Your challenge is to go out and find someone who would like to hire you and pay you to do something you would gladly do for free. Or, maybe you should be in business for yourself.

Principle #3: Successful People Have Desire

To be successful in life you've got to have desire. You've got to want something. You've got to crave something. You've got to long for something. You've got to have a burning passion. You've got to be able to answer the question: "How badly do I want it?"

But desire is only a feeling. It's of no value until you've turned your desire into action. You must make the decision to go out and *do* something. A burning desire to be, and to do, is the starting point from which you take off with your dream!

SUCCESS TIPS

● When you desire something so deeply that you won't take no for an answer, you're sure to succeed. The people who are most successful are those who are willing to do whatever it takes to get the job done!

● When you know what you want, you'll move heaven and earth to get it. When something is important enough to you, you won't stop until you've gotten it. Go out and turn your desire into an all-consuming passion. Learn what the power of desire feels like when it becomes an obsession.

 REMEMBER

You can't see the size of a person's heart from the outside.

When you have a burning desire, a complete and total obsession, you have more strength and power than you ever imagined. With this strength you're able to survive disappointment, discouragement, temporary defeat, criticism, and all the comments from the naysayers who will tell you you're wasting your time.

You've got to believe! If you don't believe in yourself, who will?

 SUCCESS TIP

To succeed, you must be willing to do whatever it takes to achieve your goals. You must convert your talk into action!

 REMEMBER

Things that are acquired without effort and without cost aren't appreciated. We tend to value things that come with a price. If everything in life were easy, we wouldn't have any challenges, we wouldn't experience growth, and we would all be the same. Boring!

JOHN ELWAY IS A WINNER!

The talk about John Elway, the Denver Broncos' future Hall of Fame quarterback, was that he choked during the big games. For 15 years, through three stinging Super Bowl losses (the truth is that those Broncos teams wouldn't have made it to the Super Bowl without him) and a dozen more seasons that would have broken plenty of other stars, he never gave up. He never ducked responsibility. He never blamed anyone else. He always played his best. He did everything a winner was supposed to do—except win it all.

And then John Elway found himself, and his wild card teammates, playing in Super Bowl XXXII against the defending Super Bowl champion Green Bay Packers and their MVP quarterback Brett Favre. Elway didn't throw a touchdown, and he completed only 12 of 23 passes for 123 yards. Favre, on the other hand, threw for 256 yards, completed 25 of his 42 passes, and threw for three touchdowns.

But Elway, and Denver, won with a huge 31-24 upset victory. It was Elway's 139th victory as the Broncos' quarterback. John Elway, the man who has won more games than any NFL quarterback, had finally won the Super Bowl.

Principle #4: Successful People Have Faith

In addition to having a dream and desire, you've got to have faith. You've got to *believe* that you can do it. This is what faith does for you:

- Faith gives you life.

- Faith gives you power.

- Faith is the starting point to being successful.

- Faith removes limitations.

- Faith is listening to that still small voice that speaks from deep within that tells you who you are and what you want to be.

FAITH AND HARD WORK BRING SUCCESS

1. *Desire success with a state of mind that becomes an obsession.* You must want it so badly that nothing will stop you.

2. *Create a step-by-step plan that lays out in minute detail the things you must do to become successful.*

3. *Execute your plan with patience, persistence, and perseverance.* Achieving success takes time. You've got to stick with your plan. You can't allow yourself to be distracted or change directions.

4. *Don't accept failure!*

PERSISTENCE

Nothing in the world can take the place of persistence.
Talent will not! Nothing is more common than unsuccessful men with great talent.
Genius will not! Unrewarded genius is almost a proverb.
Education will not! The world is full of educated failures.
Persistence prevails. Determination alone makes you omnipotent.

—Calvin Coolidge

Principle #5: Successful People Make Their Own Luck

You may think successful people became successful because they were lucky. But if you think that, you're dead wrong! Luck plays no part in being successful.

Successful people don't go through life hoping for a favorable break. They make their breaks themselves. They make their own luck. And that's what you should do!

Work hard to put yourself in a position to capitalize on the opportunities that come your way. Go out and seek situations that can provide you with the opportunities that will make you appear to be lucky to those who are watching from the sidelines.

ANECDOTE

When I think about luck I always visualize a baseball player patiently waiting for his pitch. He doesn't waste his swing on pitches that are outside the strike zone. He fouls off the ones that are strikes as he waits for that fastball up the middle that looks as if it's the size of a grapefruit. And when he sees that pitch coming, he takes a big swing with all his might and smacks the hell out of it.

And if that right opportunity doesn't come along today, just keep doing the things you do best, and continue to move forward.

For myself, I've found that when I continue to do all the right things, something unexpected always comes out of nowhere. And when I'm sitting around waiting for something to happen, it never does.

ROCKY: WINNING AGAINST ALL ODDS

In the early 1970s Sylvester Stallone's world came crashing down. He had moved to Manhattan and he went to auditions. Occasionally he got small parts in off-off-Broadway shows, but for the most part he just didn't get work. He hit bottom when he couldn't even get a job as an extra in the wedding scene in *The Godfather.*

So he turned to writing. He became so focused that he painted his windows black. He would watch a show on television, absorb the best part of it, and write a similar scene. After a while he began to understand the meaning of drama. He wrote many screenplays, and even sold a few.

In March 1975 he watched Muhammad Ali fight a relatively unknown boxer named Chuck Wepner. That fight gave him the idea for a movie: *Rocky.*

All of his life Sly had been captivated by the scenario of saving someone at the risk of his own life. Redemption. He would do anything that would give him a sense of accomplishment and respect from his peers. He sat down, wrote *Rocky,* sold it to a studio, and starred in the movie.

In 1976 *Rocky* received the Academy Award for Best Picture and earned Stallone Academy Award nominations for Best Actor and Best Original Screenplay. Since then Sylvester Stallone has made more than 23 movies. His *Rocky* and *Rambo* series of action adventures alone have grossed nearly $2 billion.

And who did he select to be his girlfriend/wife in the *Rocky* movies? Talia Shire, the actress who got married in the wedding scene in *The Godfather.*

THE LIFE OF A SALESMAN

I remember watching an advertisement on television several years ago. It showed an overweight, slightly bald, middle-aged man trying to make a sale. He makes one sales call after another, after another, after another. And with each he goes away empty.

We next see him sitting on a plane, going home after an unsuccessful week. He has spread his papers on the little fold-out tray and he's trying to complete his expense report with a small calculator. He looks terrible. You can see he's disappointed, frustrated, exhausted, and broke.

As he starts to fill out his form, the person sitting next to him asks if he can borrow the calculator. Before you know it, the two of them are having an intense discussion and the stranger ends up placing a large order.

Was the salesman lucky? No! Not at all. He worked very hard to put himself in a situation that could result in a sale. It just came from a rather unexpected place.

REMEMBER

The only break you can afford to rely upon is the one you make yourself.

SUCCESS TIP

There is a difference between wishing for something and being willing to go out and get it. You must *believe* that you can do it!

Principle #6: Successful People Aren't Afraid of Failure

Successful people know that nothing ever goes exactly as planned. And no matter how hard you work, sooner or later you must face the reality that you failed. You tried to do something and weren't successful. You didn't get the result you wanted.

You didn't get the job you hoped for. You didn't get the raise you deserved. You didn't close the big order. Your largest account just walked out the door. You struck out with the bases loaded. You missed the winning shot at the buzzer. There was a fly in the ointment. There was a glitch somewhere. You failed. SO WHAT!

You don't close every sale. You don't win every game. You aren't going to hit a home run every time you're up to bat. You don't always get what you want. Failure is OK. It's part of life. It should be expected.

The bigger question is: What do you do next? What do you do after you've failed?

As Frank Sinatra said:

"You pick yourself up and get back in the race. That's life . . ."

You don't feel sorry for yourself. You don't mope around. You pick yourself up and do it again and again and again until you get it right!

Failure is as much a part of life as success. Losing is as much a part of life as winning. The most important thing to think about is how can you ensure that you won't fail in the same way a second time.

Life is a series of trial-and-error experiences. We are taught something by a teacher, and then we try to do it ourselves. The first time we do it we probably don't get the results we want. So we try again, and again, and again. With practice we get better. Then we push ourselves as we try to do something that's a little bit more difficult. As we succeed, our expectations increase, and so does the satisfaction that comes from the feeling of a job well done.

So we set our sights a bit higher—to improve our results as compared to what we've done before and in relation to the results of those with whom we are competing—and we try again. We continue to push ourselves to new heights.

When we succeed, we once again raise the bar. And when we don't, we go back to work to improve our skills and talents, and try again.

That is why I feel that the subjects of success and failure are so intertwined: because it is through failure that we grow and develop as individuals. We learn through our failures. Failures show us our flaws, our imperfections, the areas in which we need improvement.

In order to achieve your goals, to fulfill your desires, to make your dreams come true, you're going to have to work. It is hard work that makes you better at what you do, and failing from time to time is just a part of life.

REMEMBER

If you're not experiencing failure, you're not working hard enough.

A THOUSAND THINGS THAT *DIDN'T* WORK

Someone once pointed out to Thomas Edison that he had failed because he had spent a lot of time and effort trying to create the electric lightbulb. Edison, on the other hand, felt that he had been successful because he had found thousands of different things that didn't work. He knew he wasn't going to stop until he found something that *did* work. Yes, we're all going to go through life and make mistakes, have failures, and not achieve the results we want. But many of these setbacks can be avoided and/or minimized by spending more time thinking and planning before starting to do something. Edison used the process of trial and error and wasn't about to quit.

LEARN FROM YOUR FAILURES

When you experience failure, take some time to reflect upon what happened. Pull out a pad of paper and start writing down the answers to these questions:

- Why did this happen?

- What could I have done differently?

- How can I do it better next time?

- What changes should I make in my strategies?

- What can I do to improve my planning and preparation?

Overcome the Fear of Failure

Failure is trying to do something and not getting the desired results. Fear of failure is something else. Fear of failure causes paralysis.

It's unfortunate, but many people go through life with a fear of failure. They're so afraid that they're going to make a mistake, that they won't do something right, that it won't be *perfect*, that they don't try to do anything at all. So what happens to them? They become paralyzed and don't do anything. And with this paralysis they lose the ability to have a rewarding, meaningful, and enjoyable life.

WHAT IS FEAR?

Fear is being afraid, it is being anxious, it is feeling that you are in danger. In life, fear can be real and/or imagined. But fear is actually nothing more than a state of mind that is subject to your control and direction. You can run away, or you can face the thing that is causing you to feel fearful. It is in facing the thing that is causing you to feel afraid that you grow as a person.

These are the six symptoms of fear:

1. **Indifference:** You write things off because you feel they aren't important. They're beneath you. You don't want to be bothered with them.

2. **Indecision:** You can't make up your mind. You don't know if you should or shouldn't do something. Or you can't decide if you should do A instead of B. So you do nothing!

3. **Doubt:** You're not certain as to what you should do. You can't make up your mind. You're apprehensive.

4. **Worry:** You feel anxious. You're uneasy. You're not *sure* you made the *right* decision. You don't feel confident.

5. **Overcautiousness:** You're excessively or overly cautious. You check everything over and over and over again. You want to make sure everything's right.

6. **Procrastination:** You put things off till later. You defer action. You wait so long to do something that the window of opportunity has opened and closed.

It's just physically impossible for someone who has a fear of failure to achieve anything, because that person has never tried. He never gave himself the opportunity to succeed.

It is in doing, trying, and experiencing things you never did before that you grow and develop. Through practice you get better and better at the things you do.

Principle #7: Successful People Don't Quit!

So far we've discussed dreams, desire, faith, and luck. Now I want to address the subject of quitting. Yes, we all have bad days. Yes, things don't always go your way. Yes, you may feel that the whole world is ganging up on you as everything appears to be going down the tubes.

But it is in these times of adversity that you draw on the strength deep inside of you and force yourself to continue moving forward. Other people have lost major accounts, have lost their jobs, have lost a loved one, have had a spouse decide it was time to leave, and a whole lot more.

However, through it all they find the stamina, willpower, energy, and courage to go on. And go on they do. For it is in facing adversity that we grow. We're forced to do things we never did before. And we do them.

During your lifetime you are sure to have setbacks, meet with temporary defeat, and perhaps experience some failure, if you haven't already. The question is: What do you do when that happens?

Quit? No way!

Just because you experienced a failure doesn't mean you should quit. What fun would life be if you did? Quitting is the easy way out. And besides, even if you do quit, where are you going to go? What are you going to do? More importantly, think about what has happened. If you never experienced failure, how would you ever learn from your mistakes? When you experience failure, this is what you should do:

- Analyze your mistakes.

- Determine what went wrong and why.

- Identify what you can do differently next time.

- Learn from your failure.

- Try again!

When defeat overtakes you, the easiest and seemingly most logical thing to do is quit. Instead, you should be determined to come back stronger next time. You should never accept defeat.

 REMEMBER

- **Failure, or a temporary defeat, creates opportunity.**

- **The only way you can fail is if you quit. So you just can't fail the last time you try.**

"There is only one answer to defeat, and that is victory."
—WINSTON CHURCHILL

Principle #8: Successful People Don't Take No for an Answer

Successful people are persistent. They don't quit. When they begin working on a task or project, they stick with it until its conclusion. They don't take NO for an answer. The basis of their persistence is Will Power. Their attitude is:

"I Will Get It Done!"

In life, everything is possible. But to succeed you've got to have a dream, you've got to have a plan, and you can't take NO for an answer.

IT *ONLY* TOOK TWELVE YEARS

H. Richard Hornberger, a thoracic surgeon, was a captain in the Army Medical Corps during the Korean War. He began writing the first of his three war novels—which he worked on for 12 years—after returning from combat. But his manuscript was rejected by one publisher after another. Finally, his book, *M*A*S*H,* was published by William Morrow in 1968. The rest, as they say, is history. The book became a movie and was the third highest grossing film in 1970. It then became one of the most popular television shows ever.

HOW DID YOU DIE

by *Edmund Vance Cooke*

Did you tackle that trouble that came your way
    With a resolute heart or cheerful?
Or hide your face from the light of day
    With a Craven soul and fearful?
Oh, a trouble's a ton, or a trouble's an ounce,
    Or a trouble is what you make it.
And it isn't the fact that you're hurt that counts,
    But only how did you take it?

You are beaten to earth? Well, well, what's that?
    Come up with a smiling face.
It's nothing against you to fall down flat,
    But to lie there—that's disgrace.
The harder you're thrown, why the higher you bounce;
    Be proud of your blackened eye!
It isn't the fact that you're licked that counts;
    It's how did you fight and why?

And though you be done to death, what then?
    If you battled the best you could;
If you played your part in the world of men,
    Why, the Critic will call it good.
Death comes with a crawl, or comes with a pounce,
    And whether he's slow or spry,
It isn't the fact that you're dead that counts,
    But only, how did you die?

Reprinted from *101 Famous Poems*
© Copyright 1903 by Edmund Vance Cooke.
Used with permission by NTC Contemporary Publishing Group.

What Have You Done with Your Life?

Now I would like you to spend some time thinking about who you are, what's important to you, what you value most, and where you want to go with your life. You can write down your thoughts on the blank lines I've included, on a pad of paper, or using your word processor.

Once you've written these lists, continue thinking about them. As additional thoughts cross your mind, add them to the appropriate list. For it is here that you will discover what you were born to do.

When you know who you are, where you want to go, and what you want to do, everything else falls into place. You find yourself being guided by this larger sense of purpose and direction. Your lifelong goals, dreams, and desires determine your career. Your career goals determine your job. Your responsibilities at work, at home, and to yourself determine what you will do each day.

What Have Been Your Major Accomplishments?

What have been your major accomplishments during your life? What were you commended for? What projects can you look back on and say, "I did a good job!"

Think in terms of what you've done, not job titles you've held. Be specific.

**THE MOST IMPORTANT THINGS I'VE ACCOMPLISHED
DURING MY CAREER AND/OR MY LIFE**

1. _____

2. _____

3. _____

4. _____

5. _____

6. _____

7. _____

8. _____

9. _____

10. _____

SOME LESSONS I'VE LEARNED WHILE ACCOMPLISHING THESE THINGS

1. _____

2. _____

3. _____

4. _____

5. _____

What Are You Most Proud Of?

What are the things you've done in your life that you're most proud of? The things that have given you the greatest satisfaction?

SOME OF THE THINGS I'VE DONE THAT I'M MOST PROUD OF

1. _____

2. _____

3. _____

4. _____

5. _____

6. _____

7. _____

8. _____

9. _____

10. _____

What Are Your Skills and Talents?

Many of the skills and talents you've learned from your current and previous work can be utilized in new opportunities. Here are some questions to ask yourself:

- What do you like to do?
- What are you good at? What are three skills you utilize every day in your current job? What skills have you used consistently in your previous positions?
- What kinds of things are you able to do easily and effortlessly?
- What do you really enjoy? When you're having a *really* good day, what skills are you utilizing?
- What gives you pleasure?
- If you had more time, what would you do with it? What skills or talents would you like to develop further?
- If you didn't have to work, how would you spend your time?

A CALL WITHIN A CALL

At the age of 12, Agnes Bojaxhiu felt the desire to become a nun. At 18 she joined the Sisters of Loretto, and a few years later found herself running a girls' school in the Indian town of Darjeeling, north of Calcutta. In 1946 she received a "call within a call." So she left her school and learned nursing skills. She began her good works among Calcutta's poor, and knew that this was where she belonged. In 1952 she persuaded Calcutta's municipal authorities to give her a shabby one-story building, which became a home for Calcutta's dying and destitute. Her undertakings continued with a home for abandoned children, a leper colony, and an old people's home. When she died at the age of 87, Agnes Bojaxhiu—better known as Mother Teresa—had become one of the most important people in the world.

Write down everything that comes to mind, including your hobbies and outside interests. Many people have been able to turn a hobby or outside interest into a very successful business. This is something you may want to list in your word processor, because I've only given space for 20 items. If you *really* give this some thought during the coming days, weeks, and months, you should be able to come up with 30, 40, or 50 items on this list.

MY SKILLS AND TALENTS

1. _____

2. _____

3. _____

4. _____

5. _____

6. _____

7. _____

8. _____

9. _____

10. _____

11. _____

12. _____

13. _____

14. _____

15. _____

16. _____

17. _____

18. _____

19. _____

20. _____

SOME LESSONS I'VE LEARNED WHILE DOING THESE THINGS

1. _____

2. _____

3. _____

4. _____

5. _____

6. _____

7. _____

8. _____

9. _____

10. _____

What Do You Value Most in Life?

What do you value most? What's really important to you?

When you know what it is you want today, it will be much easier for you to make your dreams come true. Here are some questions to think about:

- What do you value most in life?

- What makes you happiest?

- What gives you the most satisfaction and sense of fulfillment?

- What was most important to you during the past three years?

- What is most important today?

- What do you think will be most important during the next three years?

THINGS I VALUE MOST IN LIFE

1. _____

2. _____

3. _____

4. _____

5. _____

6. _____

7. _____

8. _____

9. _____

10. _____

STEP 2

Successful People Have a Master Plan of ACTion

Success starts with a dream. (If you don't have a dream, you have no reason or motivation to do anything.) Once you've dreamed your dream, you must figure out a way to make it come true. To do this you need a plan—a Master Plan of ACTion!

Why a Master Plan? Because it's impossible to succeed without one. Your Master Plan is your step-by-step guide that outlines everything you need to do to make your dreams come true.

With your Master Plan, the probability that you'll achieve your goals—in much less time and with much less effort—is greatly increased.

REMEMBER

When you fail to plan, you plan to fail. Intelligent planning is an essential ingredient for success in any undertaking.

Creating a Master Plan Saves You Time

With a Master Plan, you'll keep yourself from wasting time, energy, and money. Yes, I know planning isn't easy. We're not taught to think and plan. We're taught to do things. Everybody's *busy*. But that's not necessarily the same as being *productive*.

Today we live in a society where we do many things without thinking. We're action oriented, not planning oriented. However, it's been my experience that it's much easier to get the things you want in life when you take the time to figure out what you've got to do to get them.

 TIMESAVING TIP

Spend more time thinking and planning before you start making commitments and spending money. You'll get what you want much faster and it won't cost you as much in time or money.

I know you would rather get started and just "do it!" But let me ask you a few questions:

- If you were going to take a vacation and drive to Yellowstone National Park in Wyoming, or anyplace else for that matter, wouldn't it be helpful if you had a road map? Wouldn't it be helpful if you brought enough money, traveler's checks, and credit cards so you could purchase gasoline and food and be able to stay at a motel along the way? And let's not forget some clothing, fishing tackle, hiking gear, and sunscreen. A bit of planning in advance would certainly make the trip more enjoyable.

- If you were going to build a house, don't you think it would be helpful to have an architect draw up a set of blueprints? These drawings would show—in detail—the sizes and positions of each room in the house, as well as the material to be used in construction. Along with the blueprints, it may also be a good idea to have an estimate from the contractor so you know how much the house is going to cost. And wouldn't you like to select the paint colors for each room and the carpeting to be installed on the floors? Again, thinking and planning before money is spent will help you accomplish the things you want with a minimal amount of problems.

The point I'm trying to make with these two simple examples is that when you spend time devising your strategy and planning your course of action before you begin initiating action, your likelihood of success increases dramatically. And the probability of making a mistake—one that can be very costly in both time or money—decreases.

Put Your Plan on Paper

Plans that aren't written aren't plans! They're just thoughts and ideas floating around inside your head. As you reduce them to writing your dream begins to take shape. Each day you'll look at your Master Plan, think about what it is that you want to accomplish, and identify the things that need to be done next.

With time you'll add more items to your Master Plan, reorganize its contents, and make numerous changes. It is through this exercise that you develop a crisp focus. With a written plan your probability of success is greatly increased because you'll spend your valuable time, energy, and money doing things that keep you on track so you can get what you want.

Here are some additional things to remember:

- Great achievements come from great plans.

- Set goals that are attainable with hard work. When you've accomplished those goals, set new ones.

- You can dream all you want, but if you don't have a Master Plan, and if you don't put that Master Plan into action, you're kidding yourself, you're wasting your time, and nothing's going to happen!

 REMEMBER

As Yogi Berra once said: "If you don't know where you're going, you won't know where you are when you get there."

Creating Your Master Plan

To create your plan, you've got to put it down on paper. This is how you do it:

1. Pull out a pad of paper and start writing.

2. Itemize all the things you will need to do to achieve the things you desire.

3. Continue to add new items to the list as additional things cross your mind.

4. Be very detailed. The more information you put on the list, the more control you have. This is your guarantee that things won't slip through the cracks.

REMEMBER

God is in the details. Focus on and complete the tiny details. Your attention to detail will make the difference between being a success and being a huge success.

5. Give yourself plenty of time to think about your project. This isn't a one-day affair. It could very well take weeks, months, years, or even a lifetime.

 SUCCESS TIPS

● Many word processors, such as WordPerfect and Word, have an outline feature that enables you to organize your thoughts and ideas in different levels. I use the outline feature all the time. It makes it easy to organize my thoughts and to move items from one category or outline level to another. As you get deeper and deeper into the planning process, the outline feature becomes even more valuable.

● Create a blueprint of your dream. The more information you put on paper, the greater the probability that you'll succeed.

● Get up an hour earlier than usual and spend that time working on your Master Plan. You'll be amazed at how much you can accomplish when you give yourself an extra hour of focused, uninterrupted time to work.

Your Master Plan Is Constantly Changing

Once you've created your Master Plan, expect to make changes and modifications to it on almost a daily basis. Think of your Master Plan as a living, breathing document. It's got a life of its own. Your dreams, your visions, your imagination, and your actions bring your Master Plan to life.

As you begin to execute your Master Plan, you'll discover you made mistakes in your thinking or judgment. Other things will occur that you never considered or even imagined. You may have even based your plan on flawed ideas, assumptions, or misconceptions. This should be expected. Nothing in business or in life ever goes as planned. So expect the unexpected.

As you pursue your dream, plan to make changes and modifications on a regular basis. Think of yourself as the captain of a sailboat. You're trying to get from point A to point B, from point B to point C, and thereafter to points beyond. Every sailor knows that nothing is ever constant when you're on the water.

- The winds are always changing. They may switch directions. They may be heavy or light. There may be no winds at all, or they may be of hurricane force.

- The seas may be heavy, light, or choppy.

- The tides may be going in or out.

- The weather may be clear or stormy.

So what does the captain do? He's constantly making course corrections because of the changing winds, seas, and tides. He's constantly adjusting the trim of his sails. He remains aware of everything that is going on around him so he can make the necessary changes with a minimal amount of delay.

In the business of life, you make decisions. Based upon what is happening around you, you may choose to modify those decisions or make new ones. And like a sailor who is constantly adjusting the trim of the sails due to changes in the wind, weather, and seas, you must constantly make changes, adjustments, and modifications to your Master Plan.

As you're executing your Master Plan, expect to experience setbacks and failures in addition to your successes. Things go right, things go wrong. Some things are big problems. Others are just minor glitches or bumps in the road.

There will always be ups and downs. So what do you do? You deal with and resolve the problems as quickly as possible, think about and analyze what's happening, make some changes, and continue moving forward.

That's the beauty of having a well-thought-out Master Plan. The Master Plan enables you to navigate around many of the *known* hazards before you embark on your journey, and it gives you the flexibility to maneuver around the *unknown* hazards when they appear.

Create a Board of Directors to Help You Execute Your Master Plan

Once you've created your Master Plan, think about forming a team— your Board of Directors—of people who want to help you create and execute your Master Plan. People who want to help you make your dream come true.

Go out and share your dream, your plan, your vision, with your family, friends, relatives, colleagues at work, people you know through your business or professional life. Talk with your lawyer, your banker, and your accountant. Ask them to give you their thoughts, comments, suggestions, and opinions.

 SUCCESS TIP

Some of these people may become business partners, employees, outside advisors, or even investors.

REMEMBER

Always look for new people to meet. Whenever you speak with people, ask them who they know that you would like to meet.

SUCCESS TIP

It is through the process of speaking with people that you find those who are truly interested in helping you, contributing, and supporting you as you strive to make your dream come true.

When you speak with a person, give him or her the opportunity to shoot your plan full of holes. This forces you to find answers to the questions and issues that are being raised. It forces you to think things through even further because the person will undoubtedly point out issues, problems, and opportunities, and bring up other things that never crossed your mind.

SUCCESS TIP

As additional issues are raised, add them to your Master Plan.

The people you interact with are forcing you to defend your plan through the act of responding to their thoughts, comments, and questions. They're forcing you to think.

You want them to go hard on you. You don't want to be treated with kid gloves. If you're unable to come up with some good answers, it may be a sign that it's time to go back to the drawing board and rethink your plan.

REMEMBER

● It's better to spend time thinking through your plan of action before you make commitments that will cost you time, energy, and money.

● With a well-thought-out plan, the likelihood of success is greatly increased. If you're unable to adequately defend your plan, it may be best to rethink what you're doing. You've got to ask yourself:

"Are they right and am I wrong? Or am I right and are they wrong?" The answer is usually somewhere in between.

Speak with Many Different People

The more people you speak with, the stronger your resolve becomes. This gives you the opportunity to get lots of thoughts, comments, reactions, and ideas about your dream. Through these conversations you'll separate the helpers and supporters from the naysayers.

SUCCESS TIP

Keep notes of your conversations inside ACT!. Every person in an ACT! database has his own notepad, which is a great place to record notes of conversations. Over time you can review your notes and use them to help evaluate the contributions each person has made. I explain how to use ACT! in Success Steps 3 and 5.

Listen to What Everybody Has to Say

Listen to what everybody has to say about your dream and your Master Plan of ACTion. I'm certain you won't agree with all of these thoughts, comments, and ideas, but they will definitely offer you insights and observations you haven't thought about or considered. Through their contributions the probability of your succeeding is greatly increased.

REMEMBER

You're not looking for someone who agrees with you. You're looking for someone who will be honest with you. Someone who wants to help you and is willing to make a contribution to your effort.

And when you speak with people who are not supportive, think about why they aren't in agreement with you, even if you don't plan to have any further contact with them. Do they see things that you don't? Do they have a frame of reference or perspective that is different from yours? Are they looking at your dream through different-colored glasses? Ask them probing questions. Give them the opportunity to tell you what they think you're doing wrong and what you should do differently.

REMEMBER

To be successful you need the help and assistance of other people. You can't do it alone. Furthermore, it's impossible to be totally objective about things you're personally involved with.

Get Rid of the Naysayers

And then there's another group of people. These are the ones who will be very critical of the things you're trying to accomplish. They just don't understand what you're trying to do. And from their perspective it's not worth doing. It can't be done. There's no use in even trying.

When you meet such people, don't waste your valuable time and energy trying to convince them that you *can* do the things you want to do. Just walk away. Leave them alone. Look for someone else with whom you can share your dream.

What Can You Do for Each Other?

Here are a couple of additional things you should think about before you ask anyone to become a member of your team:

- What contributions can each of these people make?

- What are their specific areas of training or expertise?

- How can their skills, talents, and experience help you get to where you want to go?

- What do you have to offer them in return for their cooperation and their contributions?

- What can you do to help them make their dreams come true?

What Do You Want?

Throughout Success Step 2 I've discussed the things successful people do to become successful. Once you grasp the concepts, achieving success isn't that difficult. It's a process that every person who has became successful has followed. These are the three basic requirements:

1. You've got to have a dream.

2. Your desire must be strong enough to motivate you to create a Master Plan.

3. Your Master Plan must be executed.

With this in mind, what do you want more than anything else in life?

I Want: _____

I Want: _____

I Want: _____

- How badly do you *really* want it?

- Are you willing to sit down and create a Master Plan?

- Once you've created your Master Plan, are you willing to follow it through so you can get the things you want?

- Are you willing to put in the hard work and effort it will take to achieve your goal and make your dream come true?

 REMEMBER

- You won't be motivated to do anything if you're satisfied, if you're content, if you're happy with the way things are!

- Stay focused on your goals. Once you know where you want to go, you will continue in the right direction.

YOU'VE GOT TO PAY THE PRICE?

Every day I hear people saying, "You've got to pay the price to be successful!" I think they've got it backward. You pay the price when you're *not* successful. You pay the price when you don't accomplish the things you are capable of accomplishing. You pay the price when you don't work hard. You pay the price when you don't push yourself to the limit. You pay the price when you don't develop the skills and talents God gave you. You pay the price when you don't make something of yourself. All you've got to show for your lack of effort is a bunch of lame excuses. Yes, you truly pay a price.

When you want to do something, to accomplish something, to improve yourself, it takes time, hard work, and effort. Nothing in life is free. Nothing in this life comes easy! Everything comes with a price.

When you've accomplished your goals and fulfilled your dreams, you haven't paid a price, you've been rewarded. You've won the prize!

STEP 3
Successful People Get Results

People don't become successful simply because they put in a lot of hours. They don't become successful simply because they expend a lot of hard work and effort.

They become successful because they get the important things done. They become successful by producing high-quality work and delivering it on time. They become successful because they dot their i's and cross their t's. They become successful because they get results.

To be successful in any endeavor, you *must* do the things you're supposed to do, do them well, and get them done on time!

REMEMBER

If you *really* want to get ahead, be the best at getting the tasks that need to be done, done! Do them right and do them now! Don't put off until tomorrow what can be done now!

Clean Up the Clutter

My specialty is teaching busy people how to get organized, save time, and make more money. I help them convert at least an hour of otherwise wasted time into time that can be used more efficiently and effectively each day. In addition, they're able to focus their time, effort, and energies on the tasks and projects that are most important. The ones that will have the biggest payoff.

This gives them a two-edged sword:

1. They have more productive time available to them during the course of the day.

2. They're able to use this time to tackle their most important work, tasks, and projects.

As a result they're able to get more things done in less time and with less effort, and make more money. This is the road to success.

Many years ago I realized that most people don't get their work done on time because they lose track of whatever it is they're supposed to do. They forget about tasks and projects. They forget to make or return phone calls. They don't follow up in a timely manner on letters, memos, or proposals that they mailed. They don't get things done on time. Sometimes they don't even get things done at all!

They don't have control of their business. Their business doesn't even have control of them. Their business is out of control. Instead of working on the tasks, projects, and opportunities that have the greatest payoff, they spend the majority of their time putting out fires or doing insignificant and meaningless tasks. At the end of the day they're so exhausted they don't have the energy—mental or physical—left to do some long-term thinking and planning, let alone tackle an important project. Yes, they're very busy. They're working very hard. But they aren't getting results.

So where should you start? With the top of your desk!

Cleaning Off Your Desk

What does your desk look like? Is it neat and orderly, or do you have piles of papers strewn everywhere? Have your in- and out-boxes become *hold* boxes? Do you have sticky notes all over the place as reminders of things to-do or people to call?

If you answered yes to any of these questions, you have a typical office. It seems everybody in corporate America has a cluttered desk. But I would like to ask you a simple question: Why do we leave all of these things lying around?

The answer is simple. We leave these pieces of paper, file folders, and notes of things to-do or people to call on the tops of our desks as reminders. We're saying to ourselves: "If I see it, I'll remember to do it." Unfortunately, these reminders are often lost, forgotten, or buried in a pile. Our tasks only get our attention when the telephone rings, or there's a knock on the door, and someone is asking for that letter, memo, or report that was due days or weeks earlier. Now we must drop everything, our whole day goes up in smoke, and we don't even realize we're guilty of arson.

You probably don't realize it, but at least 60 percent of the papers on most people's desks—yours included—can be tossed. In addition, 80 percent of the stuff in the desk drawers can go.

TIMESAVING TIP

When you remove the things you no longer need, you can focus on the things that are most important.

Tools of the Trade

The process of getting organized is easy. And once you get organized you'll find that it's easy to stay that way. You'll need to do the following three things in preparation for getting rid of the clutter in your office:

1. **Block Off at Least an Hour of Uninterrupted Time.** Schedule an appointment with yourself and write it on the calendar. Most people can clean off their desks in about 60 to 90 minutes. However, if you've got a lot of stuff, it may be necessary to schedule a second or a third appointment in order to complete the job.

2. **Allow No Interruptions.** When the big day comes, close the door if you're lucky enough to have one—otherwise put a Do Not Disturb sign across the entrance to your workspace—and

turn off the telephone so you won't be interrupted. These are two great time-saving tips. Do them regularly and you'll get twice as much done in half the time with half the effort.

3. **Bring a Dumpster.** At least 60 percent of the stuff on your desk can be tossed. Before you know it your wastebasket will be filled.

Cleaning Up the Mess in Four Easy Steps

When the big day comes, these are the steps you follow:

1. **Pick Up a Piece of Paper on Your Desk.** Any piece is OK. I'm sure you have many to choose from. Look at the paper and ask yourself these questions:

   ● What is it?

   ● Why do I have it?

   ● What am I going to do with it?

   If you can't come up with some good answers, throw it away! (You can also put it in the recycling bin or pass it on to someone else.)

2. **List Your Tasks on Your Master List.** If there's work to do, note the task on your Master List. (Using your Master List is discussed later in this Success Step.)

   Your purpose is to organize your workspace. You want to go through all of the papers, files, and other miscellaneous things that have been sitting on your desk for days, weeks, months, and/or years. Think of this process as sifting and sorting. When you discover something that needs your attention—a letter you've got to respond to, a presentation you've got to work on, or a phone call you need to return—just note it on your Master List and keep going.

3. **FTP: File It, Toss It, or Pass It On.** After you've noted the task on your Master List, put the piece of paper in a file folder if you need to keep it. If you don't need it, pass it on to someone else, send it to central filing, throw it away, or put it in the recycling box. (Setting up your Master Filing System is discussed later in this Success Step.)

4. Go Through Each Piece of Paper One by One. Continue going through each piece of paper on your desk one at a time until all the piles are gone.

When you've finished going through the piles on your desk, work your way through your in- and out-boxes. And don't forget to go through all those sticky notes that are tacked to the wall and computer monitor. (Isn't that the *real* reason we own computers?) If you're really motivated, you can then tackle the piles on the credenza, the window ledges, and any other place where they may be growing and multiplying.

In no time at all you'll convert a desk that looks like a toxic waste dump into something that resembles the flight deck of an aircraft carrier. So much stuff will have been tossed that your wastebasket will be filled to the brim, overflowing, and spilling onto the floor.

When you're finished you'll have a small stack of file folders that hold the papers you need to keep. Your Master List of things to-do will be one or two pages in length. And all that will remain on the top of your desk will be a pad of paper, your telephone, and your computer. The rest will be filed, passed on to someone else, recycled, or thrown away.

Now wasn't that easy!

Organizing Your Desk Drawers

Once you've gotten rid of the piles of papers and files that were sitting on the top of your desk, it's time to clean out the drawers inside your desk.

From the things I've seen, you would think people were running a museum, a five-and-dime store, or an antique warehouse. There are boxes of Kleenex, articles of clothing, athletic apparel, napkins, plastic eating utensils, cans of food—I never realized how many packets of ketchup would fit in a desk drawer. There are daybooks going back decades and files that belonged to the desk's previous occupant—and the current occupant has been sitting at the desk for one, two, or three years.

Yes, everybody should have a junk drawer in his desk. But do *all* the drawers have to be junk drawers?

Clean Out Your Desk File Drawer

In most desks there's a drawer that's designed to hold file folders and other papers. But most people don't use these drawers for their intended purpose. Here are three reasons why:

1. They know that if they put something inside the drawer, they'll never find it again.

2. They fear that if they put a paper or file away they'll forget that there's work to be done.

3. The drawers are already filled beyond capacity, so there's no room for anything more.

REMEMBER

People leave things on the tops of their desks as reminders of things to-do.

It's been my experience that 80 percent of the papers inside most people's desk drawers can be tossed. Very little is current, and most of the information is available elsewhere in the office or inside a computer. In many cases the papers haven't been looked at in a long, long time. That's because the person's important papers, documents, and records have been sitting in piles on the top of the desk. The stuff in the drawer is historical, sometimes going back to the Jurassic age.

With a little housecleaning you can get rid of the unnecessary things in this drawer. Once it's been cleaned out, you can use it to store the important files, documents, and records that have been sitting in piles on the top of your desk. For most people, this can be done in about 30 minutes. Here's how you do it:

1. **Open the desk drawer, pull out the first file folder, and place it on the top of your desk.**

2. **Go through each piece of paper in the folder one by one.** If there are papers you need to keep, put them aside in a *keeper* pile for the moment. Everything else should be tossed.

3. **Go through the keeper pile.** Put the papers in the keeper pile back in the folder, or create new folders as necessary.

TIMESAVING TIPS

● **Group related papers together with staples or paper clips. Papers that are most important, or are referred to frequently, should be placed at the front of the file. Everything else should be placed behind.**

● **If your folders are beat-up, dog-eared, and dirty, throw them away and use new folders.**

4. **Go through the next file in the drawer.** Continue the process until you've gone through and inspected each file. As you go through your files, you'll certainly discover things that need to be done and papers that are in the wrong file. Add the undone tasks to your Master List and keep working. When you find misfiled papers, simply put them in the correct file, or make a new one.

When you've finished cleaning out your desk file drawer, you'll find you've kept just a handful of files. The rest have been thrown away, given to someone else, or returned to central filing. Now you've got an empty drawer in which you can store the papers that had previously been in piles on the top of your desk.

Setting Up Your Master File Drawer

Think of the space within your Master File drawer—the drawer in your desk that's designed to hold file folders—as if it were prime real estate. Papers, documents, records, and other files that you look at frequently should be easy to get to. So place them at the front of the drawer for easy access. Things you refer to less frequently should be placed behind.

Papers, documents, and records that you need to keep but don't look at or review very often can be stored even further away, in the file drawers in the credenza or in other filing cabinets within your office or workspace. Other files can be stored in filing cabinets outside your immediate office area or in central filing. And files that *must* be kept, but may not ever be looked at again—unless there's a big problem—should be placed in transfer cases and stored in an off-site location or possibly in the basement.

There are several ways you can organize the files in your Master File drawer. Many people organize their files alphabetically, which is great if you have files on many people. But I've found it can be a bit cumbersome when you're keeping papers on numerous projects, tasks, and other things.

My preference is to organize these files by frequency of use. Files you use frequently should be placed in the front of the drawer. Other files that you refer to from time to time should be placed behind the first group. And files that are reviewed infrequently can be stored elsewhere.

 TIMESAVING TIP

Before you store things in transfer cases and place them in semi-permanent storage, create a list of the contents of each box. Tape a copy of that list to the outside of the box, place another copy inside the box, and keep a copy in a file within your office.

Setting Up Your Master Filing System

This is how you set up your Master Filing System within your Master File drawer:

- **Use New File Folders.** The first thing you need is a brand-new box of manila file folders. Don't waste your valuable time trying to reuse an old file folder. When a file folder is beat-up, dog-eared, and dirty, just replace it. Your time is much too valuable to waste trying to reuse a folder that cost less than a nickel when it was new.

- **Use Letter-Size Files.** Letter-size file folders are much easier to use than legal-size folders. Ninety-nine percent of the papers that go into files are letter-size or smaller, so don't waste the extra money purchasing legal folders. Besides, legal folders take up an extra 20 percent of the space in a file drawer.

- **Use File Folders with Three Tabs.** Use folders that have three tabs across the top—left, center, and right—also referred to as third-cut files. When you put these files inside the drawer (they should be collated) you're able to see three file labels at a time. This makes it easier to locate papers inside the file drawer. You'll save time because you're able to find your file in seconds.

TIMESAVING TIP

You may not realize it, but most people lose an hour a day looking for papers that are lost on the tops of their desks.

- **Write File Labels by Hand.** To make life easier, keep a supply of folders in your desk drawer. When you need a new file, pull one out of the drawer and write your file label by hand. Don't waste your time typing gummed labels. Though typed file labels may look pretty and attractive, creating them is a rather time-consuming process, especially when you're typing a single label.

TIMESAVING TIP

If you want to color-code your file folders—it's often easier to locate files when you're looking for a color instead of a specific file label—use colored markers instead of the gummed labels that have the colored bars across the top or colored folders. With the colored markers, just draw a line across the top of the file tab or across the file label itself.

- **Use Expandable File Pockets Instead of Hanging Folders.** Many people use hanging files in their file drawers for the sole purpose of keeping their manila folders from falling over. Unfortunately, the hanging folders themselves can take up 30 percent or more of the space within an empty file drawer.

  As an alternative to using these hanging files, use expandable file pockets, also called accordion files. These are available in expansions of 3½ and 5¼ inches. Just put the manila file folders inside the expandable file pockets and place the expandable file pockets inside the file drawer.

PRINT YOUR LABELS WITH A LABEL PRINTER

If you've ever printed labels from your laser printer, you know it's easy to print a whole page of them. But what do you do when you need to print just one label? I hope you're not still using a typewriter. If you are, I've got a better idea. Use a label printer.

Seiko makes a very good label printer, the Smart Label Printer Pro. The SLP Pro quickly prints laser-quality labels on a variety of label sizes, incorporating text, photolike graphics, special messages, and bar codes. So get rid of your typewriter and use your computer to type all of your labels. You'll save yourself hours of time. For more information contact:

- *Seiko Instruments USA, Inc.*, 1130 Ringwood Court, San Jose, CA 95131; 800-888-0817; www.seikosmart.com

---

 TIMESAVING TIPS

- Place the expandable file pockets inside your file drawer so the labels on the manila folders face you. This makes it much easer to find a specific file, because you can see your file labels.

- When you're working on a large task or project, place the papers, documents, records, and other information that make up the project in properly labeled manila folders. Then place those files inside an expandable file pocket.

Dealing with Reference Materials

As you're going through the papers on your desk, you'll undoubtedly find trade journals, newsletters, magazines, newspaper articles, and other material you want to read and/or keep. I suggest you do two things:

1. Create a reading file.

2. Create a resource file.

Setting Up a Reading File

In today's fast-paced world the quick utilization of information gives you a huge competitive advantage. So when information—a letter, memo, newsletter, magazine, trade journal, or anything else—crosses your desk, scan it quickly to see if there's anything that you can put to use immediately. If it's *really* important, read it now. Otherwise, put it inside a manila file labeled *Reading.* Then when you have some down-time during the day, you can go through the file to see what information is important to you and take a few minutes to read it.

 TIMESAVING TIPS

- When you go on a business trip, take your reading file with you. Go through the file on the plane or in your hotel room. Keep the material you need and throw the rest away.

- When you have reading material that's important or timely, note it as a task on your Master List. That way you won't forget about it.

Read with a Pen in Your Hand

Every time you read a letter, memo, report, presentation, newsletter, newspaper, magazine, or anything else, always keep a fine-tipped pen or highlighter handy. Circle, underline, or highlight the sentences or paragraphs that catch your attention as you're reading. Write comments on the page or in the margins when appropriate. (If you don't want to write on the page itself, slap a sticky note on the page and write your thoughts and comments on the sticky note.) When you pick up this piece of paper at some future time, you'll know exactly what caught your attention at the time you read it.

After you've read the article or other piece of information, place it in the appropriate file or create a special file dedicated to this specific topic or subject.

When you need to keep an article from a newspaper or magazine, rip the page out and throw the rest of the publication away. If you must keep the newspaper or magazine intact, make a copy of the article and then pass the publication on to the next person.

Setting Up a Resources File

If your office is like everybody else's, you've probably got one or more stacks of newspapers, magazines, trade journals, reports, and other miscellaneous material that you feel might be of benefit at some future time. But leaving this stuff in piles doesn't do you much good. Even if the answer to the $64,000 question was buried in one of those piles, you probably wouldn't know where it was. So instead of leaving the information stacked in a pile somewhere in your office, organize it so that it's available to you when you need it.

 ANECDOTE

Every time I work with a person, we always find something that was lost on his desk that is so important its discovery more than pays for my fees.

This is what you do:

1. Go through the stack and create file folders for each topic that's important to you.

2. Place the related papers inside the folder.

3. Place the folders inside expandable file pockets and put them in a file drawer or a filing cabinet.

Now you'll be able to get your hands on valuable information when you need it and you'll also get rid of a pile of things that have been taking up space and gathering dust in your office.

 TIMESAVING TIP

Search the Internet when you have a question: As an alternative to keeping large amounts of paper in files (which can be a laborious and time-consuming task), think of the Internet as your library. When you need some specific information, just log on to one of the search engines and enter a few key words. In the blink of an eye you'll have an incredible amount of information at your fingertips. You can then download the information directly into your computer or bookmark Web sites for future reference.

Using Your Master List

You master your day with your Master List. The idea behind the Master List is that you have a complete inventory of everything that needs to be done. This isn't just a list of things to-do today or tomorrow, but a list of *everything* you need to do today, tomorrow, and well into the future.

The more detailed your Master List, the more control you have. With your Master List, it's no longer necessary to keep piles of papers on your desktop. Simply scan your list from top to bottom and you know in an instant everything you need to do, who you need to do it for, and when it must be done.

With your Master List you have complete and total control. And with a neat, orderly workspace, you're no longer working in chaos.

Here are some Master List tips:

- **Use a Big Piece of Paper.** Write your Master List on a big piece of paper. Don't write it on the back of an envelope or on a sticky note.

- **Keep Your Master List Clean.** Your Master List is a very important document. Keep it clean. Don't use it as a scratch pad, and don't doodle on it.

- **Keep Your Master List on Your Desk.** Leave your Master List on the top of the desk. This makes it easy to add new items of business and cross off completed items.

- **Write on Every Line.** A piece of paper usually has 25 to 30 lines. Use them. Don't skip lines as you add new items to your Master List.

- **Use a Fine-Tipped Pen.** Write the items on your Master List with a fine-tipped pen. Pencils smudge and will render your Master List unreadable in no time at all.

- **Don't Worry About Priorities.** Some people rewrite their things to-do lists every morning so as to get the most important items on their list at the top of the page. I think this is a waste of time. That's the beauty of using your Master List. Just scan the list from top to bottom to identify the most important task that needs to be done. With this method you'll complete your *important* work—and get results—instead of wasting your valuable time rewriting a list.

● **Look at Your Master List Throughout the Day.** Keep your Master List on the top of your desk and refer to it all day long. Your objective is to get your most important work done. These are the tasks and projects that are worth big money and that will have a huge payoff.

● **Cross Off Completed Tasks.** When you've completed a task, draw a line through it. (A check mark in the margin isn't gratifying enough.)

● **Tackle New Tasks.** When you finish one task, look at your Master List and ask yourself: "What is the most important task that I should tackle next?" Don't think about it. Do it!

REMEMBER

Your goal is *not* to try to get all the miscellaneous items off your Master List so you can then begin working on the hard ones. Your goal is to tackle your most important tasks—those that take time, thought, consideration, and energy—while you have plenty of lead time. With this approach you'll produce high-quality work, get it done on time with less strain, tension, and effort, and have better results.

● **Add New Items of Business to Your Master List.** As new items of business come up throughout the day—the phone rings, the mail arrives, or you receive an e-mail message—don't drop whatever you're doing just to get this new task out of the way. Simply add it to your Master List and continue doing whatever you were doing.

TIMESAVING TIP

One of the biggest impediments to being a success in business is interruptions. If you allow your flow of work to be interrupted every time the phone rings, the mail arrives, or someone walks through the door, you'll never get anything done. It's OK to turn off your phone and close the door (or put up a Do Not Disturb sign) for short periods of time so you can complete your important work.

- **Start a Second Page.** When you've used up all the lines on the first page of your Master List, start a second page.

- **Consolidate the Pages of Your Master List.** When you've completed about 50 percent of the items on the first page of your Master List, it's time to rewrite the list so as to consolidate all the items on one page. If you don't, you'll end up with a pile of lists.

  Go through each item on the first page of your Master List and rewrite the task on the newest page. After you rewrite the item, draw a line through it. When you're finished, look over the entire list to make sure every item on the page has been completed or transferred. You can then throw the list away or put it in a file labeled *Old Lists*.

 TIMESAVING TIP

Always date your papers. This enables you to see how long you've had something or determine where it falls within a chronology of events. It will also tell you how long something's been hanging around on your Master List.

- **Plan for Tomorrow.** At the end of the day, look over your Master List before you go home and ask yourself: "What is the most important task I should work on tomorrow?" Schedule an appointment with yourself, write it on your calendar, and do the task first thing in the morning. (This is another great time-saving tip.)

DON'T BE AFRAID OF A LONG MASTER LIST

Many people become terrified when they have a long list of things to-do. They think they've got to complete each and every task by the end of the day, and when they don't, they feel frustrated. My approach is a bit different. I want to list *everything* that I've got to do on my Master List, because that guarantees that I won't forget about anything. On any given day I've got between 100 and 150 things to-do or people to call.

Now I don't want you to think I get all of these items done each day, because I don't. That isn't my purpose. My goal is to make sure I get the *important* things done every day. Some days I may only get to cross one item off my Master List. But that one item was the most important task I needed to complete, so I had a very productive day.

My suggestion is that you get in the habit of recording *everything* you need to do on your Master List. You'll get more things done in less time and with less effort, the quality of your work will improve, and you'll find that you have much more control over your life.

Put Your Master List Inside Your Computer

In 1984 I started my time management consulting firm and began teaching people how to get organized, clean the clutter off their desks, and use their Master Lists. In the early 1990s I began research for my third book, *Winning the Fight Between You and Your Desk,* and discovered the personal computer. In my book I reviewed more than 150 pieces of productivity-improving hardware and software and found that you could do a whole lot more than simply write letters with a word processor or crunch numbers with a spreadsheet.

Of all the programs I reviewed, there was one that changed my life: a contact management program named ACT!. Once I discovered I could put my Master List inside my computer I became an ACT! addict.

Now, the concept of keeping track of things to-do on a Master List is rock solid. It is built upon a very firm foundation. However, there is one drawback. It is done manually using a pencil and a piece of paper.

With ACT! I could keep track of all my activities—my calls, meetings, and things to-do—electronically and leverage the power of my computer. It was no longer necessary to use a pencil and a piece of paper. With a simple, easy-to-use, off-the-shelf piece of software I was able to throw away my obese Rolodex file, my tattered name and address book, and the leather-bound daily planning book I had used for a decade.

Today, with ACT!'s help, I'm able to do the work of five or six people all by myself without ever leaving the comfort of my own home.

I would like to mention that I don't work for Symantec, ACT!'s publisher, and I don't own stock in the company. I'm just an everyday user who thinks ACT! is a very good productivity-improving tool. Well, to be honest, I'm no longer just an everyday user. I've now written three ACT! books, the newest being *ACT! 4 for Windows for Dummies*. And I have an ACT! newsletter, *ACT! in ACTion*. (If you would like a free sample issue, you can fill out the online form at my Web site, www.ACTnews.com, or fill out the response card at the back of this book.)

ACT! ISN'T THE ONLY CONTACT MANAGER AVAILABLE

There are many good contact managers available—Goldmine, Maximizer, and Sharkware, to name a few—but for myself, I like ACT!. If you're using another contact management program, please read this part of the book because it does have some useful information. And if you're not using a contact management program, you should go out and get one today!

ACT! is published by Symantec Corporation and is available for about $200. For more information you can call Symantec customer service at 800-441-7234, or visit Symantec's ACT! Web site at www.symantec.com/act.

In this Success Step I'm going to explain how to use ACT! to automate your Master List, and in Success Step 5 I'll explain how to use ACT! to build relationships with the right people.

You Need a Place to Store Personal Information

Have you ever met a person and written some information about him on the back of his business card? What did you do with the card when you returned to the office? Put it in your Rolodex file? Put it in the person's file folder? Place it in the lap drawer of your desk?

Once you did something with this card, how did you remember to follow up with the person at some future time? The truth is, you probably didn't.

From my perspective, names and addresses written on pieces of paper are worthless. However, put them inside your computer in a contact management program like ACT! and you have a truly effective networking tool.

Today, the name of the game is:

• Who do you know?

• How well do you know them?

• How quickly can you get them on the phone?

When you meet someone, don't waste that opportunity to get to know him better.

The beauty of ACT! is that it gives you a place to store names, addresses, and phone numbers and other information for anybody and everybody. The ACT! Contact window is shown in Fig. 3.1. The following are ways you can take full advantage of information with ACT!:

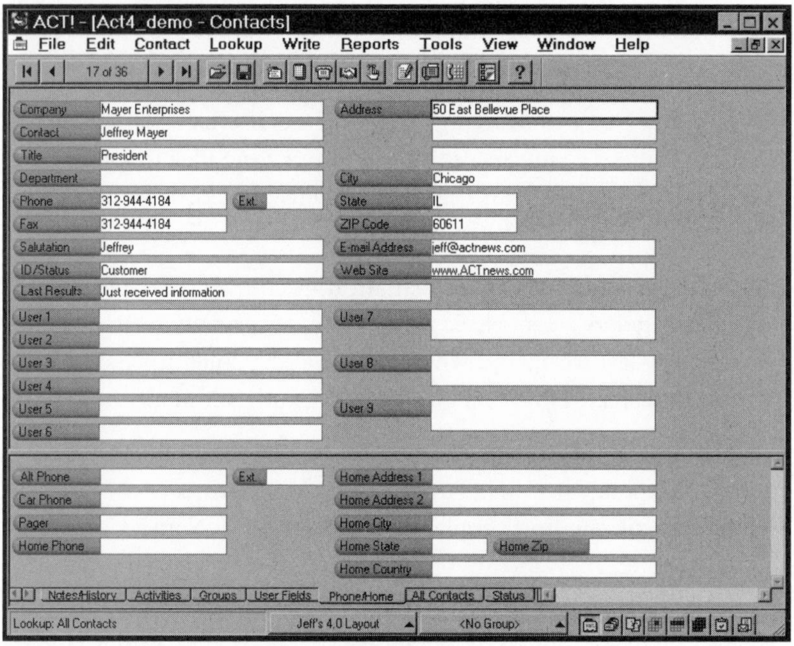

Figure 3.1 The ACT! Contact window.

- **Storing Names and Addresses:** ACT! gives you a place to store everybody's work and home address. When you need to send a letter, just click on an icon and ACT! inserts the person's name and address into a form letter template. The letter can then be printed, sent as a fax, or sent as e-mail.

  After you've sent the letter you can attach it to the person's contact record. Click on the attachment icon and ACT! opens the letter for immediate review.

- **Storing Phone and Fax Numbers:** ACT! gives you a place to store the numbers for a person's phone and fax, pager, car phone, and mobile phone. Click on an icon and ACT! even dials the phone for you. If you're using faxing software, like WinFax PRO, you can send faxes directly from ACT!.

- **Storing E-mail Addresses:** ACT! gives you a place to store a person's e-mail address. E-mail can be sent and received directly from within ACT!. The e-mail message can then be attached to the person's record for easy reference.

- **Storing Web Site Addresses:** ACT! gives you a place to store a company's Web site address. Click on the address and ACT! launches your Web browser and takes you to the selected Web site.

- **Keeping Notes of Meetings and Conversations:** When you have a meeting or a conversation it's always a good idea to jot down a brief summary of the things that were discussed. ACT! makes this easy to do because everybody has his or her own notepad.

- **Printing Reports:** Any information in your ACT! database can be printed as a report. So when your boss wants to know who you saw last week, and what you have scheduled for next week, you can create and print your report in no time at all.

- **Finding People:** Once you've entered people into ACT!, it's easy to find them with ACT!'s powerful lookup feature. In the blink of an eye, you can find people by First Name, Last Name, Company, City, State, ZIP code, and any other criteria that may come to mind. You can even search for people over the Internet and then add them to your ACT! database. Try doing that with a paper-based system.

Activities Are Scheduled with People

My Master List concept has weathered the test of time and has helped millions of people get organized. Unfortunately, there are some drawbacks to using a Master List. That's because the items are written on a piece of paper and listed by task. Here are some of the Master List's shortcomings:

• There is no way to associate a task with a specific person.

• There is no way to sort tasks by priority.

• There is no way to separate a list of calls from a list of things to-do.

• There is no way to sort tasks by date.

The Master List is just items listed on a piece of paper.

But once you've added a person to your ACT! database, you automate your Master List and bring the power of your computer into play. Now you can do some amazing things, because each activity—a call, meeting, or thing to-do—is associated with a person.

To schedule an activity, just click on an icon and the Schedule Activity box, shown in Fig. 3.2, pops up. This is what you can do from within the Schedule Activity box:

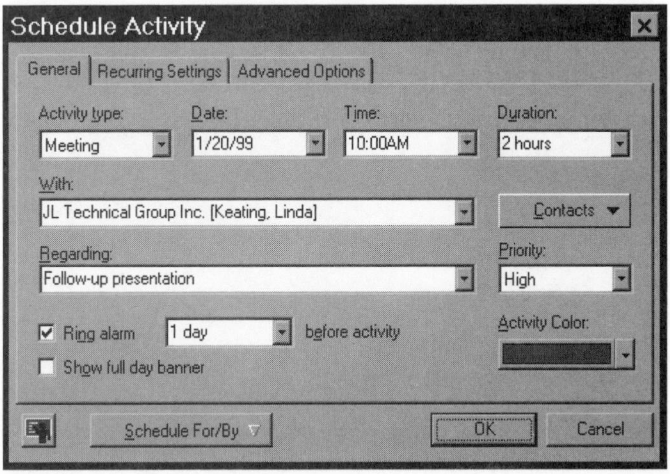

Figure 3.2   Schedule Activity box.

- Select the type of activity—a Call, Meeting, or To-do.

- Choose the activity's Date, Time, and Regarding Information.

- Set the Duration of an activity.

- Assign a Priority.

- Set an Alarm, and assign a Lead Time so you will be reminded of the activity.

- Schedule Recurring activities.

- Schedule activities with other users on the network.

View Your Tasks in Many Different Ways

Once you've scheduled your activities you can view them in many different ways.

View Your Activities by Person

Click on an icon and you can view all the activities you've scheduled with a particular person. For instance, if I want to see all the things I need to do, or follow up on, with Linda Keating (Linda's a very good friend and an ACT! Certified Consultant in Palo Alto, California), I find her in the database and click the Activities tab (Fig. 3.3), and the list of everything that's pending with her appears.

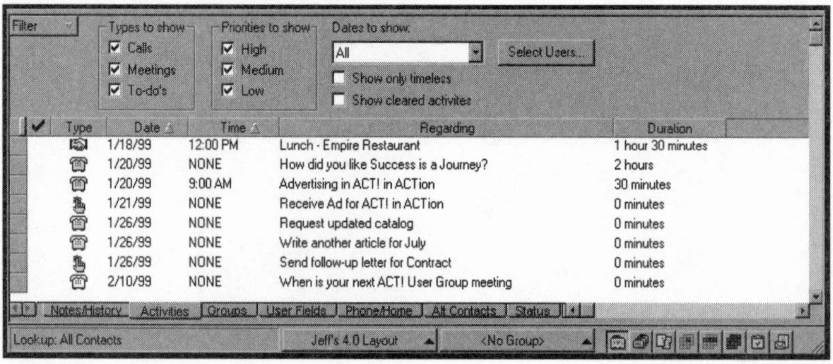

Figure 3.3 ACT!'s Activities tab.

This is a very powerful feature. When you're speaking with an important customer, client, or prospect—or even your boss or supervisor—about one issue, you can also follow up or discuss other pending items. This increases your productivity and saves you time, because you've always got a complete list of the things that are going on between you and everybody in your life. It also enables you to avoid playing long games of telephone tag.

SUCCESS TIP

Put everybody you know into ACT! and you can replace your big, fat, obese Rolodex file and the name and address book you've been using for the last decade.

One day as I was working with a client named Mike, I explained to him that with a click of his mouse he could view a list of all the calls, meetings, or things to-do that were pending with each person in his ACT! database. This list of tasks could be viewed by person, as a list, or in a calendar view. As I was describing these features Mike's eyes opened wide and then a huge ear-to-ear grin appeared on his face. This was the cat's meow.

Mike then told me he was very frustrated because he wasted a lot of time playing telephone tag with his direct reports. He would call and leave a message. They would return his call and leave a message. And finally, the parties would actually speak to each other and discuss the specific item of business that was on Mike's mind. The following morning a new item would appear on his desk from his assistant's tickler file and another round of calls and callbacks would be initiated.

With ACT! that doesn't happen any longer. Whenever Mike has a follow-up item, or something crosses his mind that he wants to follow up on, he schedules it inside ACT!. Now he's got a list of every item that is open with everybody in his life, both business and personal. The only thing he has to do is click on an icon. Now he's being productive!

View Your Activities as a List

Click on another icon and you can view your calls, meetings, and things to-do as a list. ACT!'s Task List, shown in Fig. 3.4, is basically the same as my Master List. But there's a huge difference between the two. The Master List is maintained on a piece of paper, while the Task List is maintained electronically from inside the computer.

With the Task List you can see all the things that need to be done in a list view. Because the list is compiled electronically, your increase in productivity is phenomenal. These are some of the things you can do:

- **View Activities by Date.** With the click of a button you can view activities for today, tomorrow, or any date or range of dates in the past or the future.

- **View Activities by Priority.** Activities can be viewed by priority and can even be color-coded.

Type	Date	Time	Priority	Scheduled With	Regarding	Duration
☎	1/20/99	NONE	Low	Mitzi Bouffard	Mobile phone service - Peggy Collins	0 minutes
☎	1/20/99	NONE	Low	David Rechs	ACT! 4 for Windows for Dummies	0 minutes
☎	1/20/99	NONE	Low	Linda Keating	When is your next ACT! User Group meeting	0 minutes
☎	1/20/99	NONE	Low	Stephen Del Grosso	What's going on.	0 minutes
☎	1/20/99	NONE	Low	Steve Chipman	Write article for ACT! in ACTion Newsletter	0 minutes
☎	1/20/99	NONE	Low	Bud Rice	Write article for ACT! in ACTion Newsletter	0 minutes
✉	1/20/99	NONE	Low	Tom Huffman	Order new catalog from National Paper	0 minutes
👤	1/20/99	NONE	Low	Mitzi Bouffard	Send Success is a Journey	0 minutes
👤	1/20/99	NONE	Low	Gloria Lenares	Call traffic about distribution	0 minutes
👤	1/20/99	NONE	Low	Greg Thomas	Prepare presentation for 1st quarter	0 minutes
👤	1/20/99	NONE	Low	Linda Keating	Receive Ad for ACT! in ACTion	0 minutes
☎	1/20/99	NONE	Low	Lon Orenstein	Thank you for order	30 minutes
☎	1/20/99	NONE	Low	Jeff Nelson	Contract negotiations	2 hours
✉	1/20/99	8:00 AM	Low	David Ashley	Breakfast Meeting	30 minutes
☎	1/20/99	9:00 AM	Low	Linda Keating	Write article for ACT! in ACTion Newsletter	30 minutes
✉	1/20/99	10:00 AM	Low	Andy Kaplan	Follow-up presentation	30 minutes
☎	1/20/99	11:00 AM	Low	Carolyn Kilpatrick	ACT! 4 for Windows for Dummies	45 minutes
✉	1/20/99	12:00 PM	Low	Bob Cox	Lunch - Empire Restaurant - Show New Products	1 hour
✉	1/20/99	1:30 PM	Low	Mitzi Bouffard	Follow-up presentation for Harold Collins account	1 hour
✉	1/20/99	3:00 PM	High	Steve Chipman	Presentation for new products	1 hour 30 minutes
✉	1/20/99	6:30 PM	Low	Bill Stankey	Meet For Dinner at Gibson's	3 hours

Figure 3.4   ACT!'s Task List.

- **View Activities by Task.** You can view your list of calls, meetings, and things to-do as a group, or individually.

- **Re-sort Your Activities.** Each column in the Task List can be re-sorted in ascending or descending order by just clicking on the column heading. This enables you to sort by date, by task, by person, or by activity.

View Your Activities on a Calendar

If you're a visual person and are most comfortable looking at your scheduled calls, meetings, and things to-do in a calendar view, just click one of the calendar icons and your activities are displayed in a Daily, Weekly, or Monthly calendar view. The daily calendar is shown in Fig. 3.5.

In these views you have the same filtering options that are available in the Task List window.

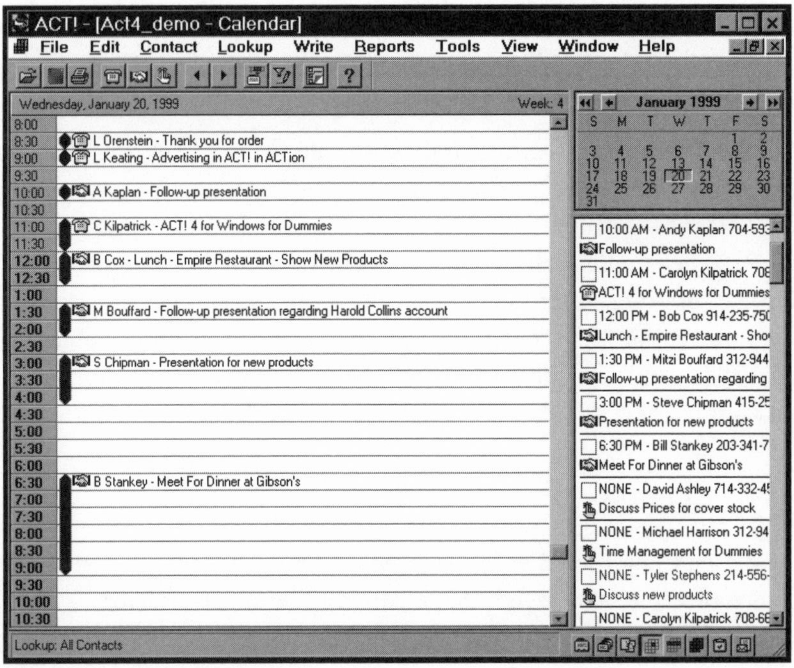

Figure 3.5   Daily calendar.

The Power to Modify Activities

Once you've scheduled an activity, it's very easy to change the activity's particulars. This is very important because most businesspeople don't do a very good job of following up with their customers, clients, prospects, or opportunities.

Let me ask you a few questions:

- What happens when you mail a proposal to someone and say in the letter that you'll call in a few days? How do you remember to make the call? Do you call on the day you say you will? Do you call within two weeks of sending the letter? Have you ever forgotten to make the call?

- What happens when people say they'll send you something? How do you remember to follow up with them if the item isn't received within the next few days?

- How do you remember to call people when they ask you to follow up in 30, 60, 90, or 180 days?

- How do you keep on top of work that has been delegated to someone else?

No, ACT! won't make the follow-up calls for you. But it will make sure you don't forget that the calls should be made.

This is how you put ACT! to work for you: As you're signing a letter, just click on the Call icon and the Schedule Activity dialog box (see Fig. 3.2) appears. Enter the call's specifics—the date, time, and regarding information (if you like, you can also set an alarm and/or assign a priority)—and click OK. When the correct day arrives, the call appears on your list of activities. What could be simpler!

 TIMESAVING TIP

A good follow-up system is one of the most important tools you need in order to be successful. This is how you stay on top of things.

REMEMBER

Ninety percent of being successful is just showing up.

Automatically Roll Over Your Unfinished Activities from One Day to Another

With a paper-based system, unfinished tasks need to be consolidated on a new page when the Master List or things to-do list is 50 to 60 percent completed. If this isn't done, you end up with a pile of lists, and older tasks just slip through the cracks.

Or, if a daily planning book is being used, unfinished tasks must be rewritten from one day's page to another. If they aren't, they will soon be forgotten.

(And what happens to all the wonderful information that was written on the pages of the daily planning book at the end of the year? It's gone! The old pages are replaced with new ones and are put inside a box or file drawer, never to be looked at again.)

With ACT!'s auto-rollover feature you'll never forget an unfinished task. When you turn on your computer and start ACT!, every unfinished task from a previous day is automatically rolled over to the current date. This feature ensures that no unfinished tasks will ever be left behind.

However, if you don't want to use the auto-rollover feature, you can view all of your previously scheduled but not completed tasks by opening the Task List and selecting the Past option.

Rescheduling Activities Is Easy

Successful people are persistent. The difference between successful people and everybody else is that successful people don't take NO for an answer.

In business, the easiest way to blow someone off is to tell him to call you back tomorrow, next week, or in a few months. Most people never get around to making that call again. They lose track of the file or their cover letter, or they just plain forget about it.

With ACT! that just doesn't happen. When someone tells you to call back in a week, a month, or even a year, all you've got to do is change the activity's date. Just click on an icon, a calendar appears, and you change the date and click OK. No muss, no fuss. A week, month, or year later this activity appears at the top of your list of people to call.

TIMESAVING TIP

When you speak with someone and he asks you to call back in 20 minutes, just set an alarm. Twenty minutes later ACT! reminds you to make the call.

You Can Take It with You

If you're like most businesspeople, you probably spend more than half your time away from your office. But just because you're away from your desk doesn't mean you have to be out of touch. When you leave the office you can take your ACT! information with you in many different formats.

- **Take Your Notebook Along.** Many people travel with their notebook computers. In fact, for many people a notebook has replaced the traditional desktop PC. When they leave the office, they put their notebook in their briefcase and they're off to their next meeting or business trip. When they return, they just slip the notebook into a docking station and they're back in business.

  If you work this way, your ACT! database is portable. Take your notebook on a business trip, and you bring your entire ACT! database along for the ride.

  With ACT!'s synchronization capability, you can synchronize your notebook's database with the ACT! database on your company's local area network (LAN) when you return to the office. Through the synchronization process, any changes you made to your ACT! database will also be made to the ACT! database on the LAN. And any changes made to the LAN's database will automatically be reflected in your notebook.

- **Use a Palmtop Computer.** Many people prefer to use a palmtop computer because palmtops are very powerful, yet weigh less than a pound and are the size of a paperback book. Programs are now available that enable you to move ACT! information from your notebook and/or desktop PC to the most popular palmtop computers. ACT! links are available for 3Com's PalmPilot, Franklin's REX, Sharp's Mobilon, and other palmtop computers that utilize the Windows CE platform.

● **Print Your Information Out on Paper.** If you can't live without your leatherbound daily planning book, any information in your ACT! database can be printed on pages that fit any size daily planning book.

STEP 4

Successful People
Take Responsibility
for Their Time

Successful people put a high value on their time. They don't waste it. They realize that time is the most valuable asset they have, so they do everything they can to get maximum results.

If you want to get ahead in life, you can't afford to waste time. You've got to get the most out of each day. You've got to complete your work, tasks, and projects on time, do them well, and do them right. In this Success Step you'll discover dozens of time-saving tips, techniques, ideas, and strategies that will help you get more out of each day.

IT'S THE ONLY GAME WE'RE PLAYING

Before every game, just after the national anthem was played, someone on a certain Major League baseball team would yell: "Hey, this is a really big game, guys."

"Why's that?" someone else would ask.

"Because it's the only one we're playing," a third person would shout.

During the months that ritual was followed, the team had the best won-lost record in the National League.

Increase the Value of Your Time

We've all heard the phrase "Time is money." But what does that *really* mean? It means that the things you know—your skills, talents, knowledge, and experience—have value and that someone is willing to pay you for them. So when you're not fully utilizing your God-given skills, talents, knowledge, and experience, you are indeed wasting money.

If I may, I would like to ask you a question: How much value do you put on your time?

REMEMBER

Your skills, talents, knowledge, and experience are the most valuable—and the only—assets you've got.

SUCCESS TIP

Make the most of your God-given talents, and you'll be compensated beyond your wildest dreams.

The greater the value you put on your time, your skills, and your talents, the more you're going to accomplish, because you will utilize them better. You'll reach your goals and achieve your dreams sooner. And when those goals have been reached, you'll set your sights on even bigger ones.

TREASURE EVERY MOMENT

To realize the value of one year: Ask a student who failed his final exam.

To realize the value of one month: Ask a mother who has given birth to a premature baby.

To realize the value of one week: Ask the editor of a weekly newspaper.

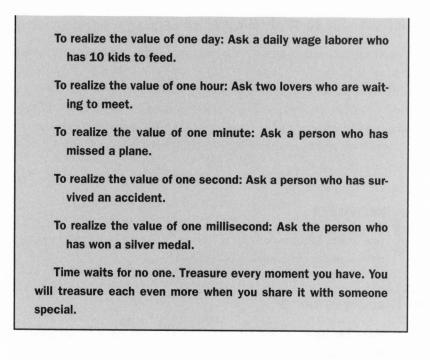

To realize the value of one day: Ask a daily wage laborer who has 10 kids to feed.

To realize the value of one hour: Ask two lovers who are waiting to meet.

To realize the value of one minute: Ask a person who has missed a plane.

To realize the value of one second: Ask a person who has survived an accident.

To realize the value of one millisecond: Ask the person who has won a silver medal.

Time waits for no one. Treasure every moment you have. You will treasure each even more when you share it with someone special.

Give Yourself a Raise

Put a higher value on your time and you'll spend it differently. Learn how to use your time more effectively and you'll accomplish a lot more and make a lot more money.

In order to accomplish more in your life, you've got to perform at a higher level. Yes, there are only 24 hours in a day, and I know you spend somewhere between 8 and 10 of them working. (And if you add commuting time, you've probably got a 10-, 12-, or even 14-hour day.)

So I'm not going to ask you to put in any more hours. I just want to ask you a question: "How do you spend those 8 to 10 working hours?" Well, I'm going to show you how to improve the way you spend your time so that you'll accomplish much more every day, and in the end have more time for your family, your friends, and yourself.

For the fun of it, let's pretend that someone is willing to pay you $600 an hour for your skills, talents, knowledge, and experience. Multiply that out. Eight hours a day is $4800. Five days a week is $24,000. And 50 weeks a year (you do get a vacation) is $1,200,000. Now we're talking *real* money.

And I'm sure you work 10 or even 12 hours a day, and probably on Saturdays and parts of Sundays, so these figures are on the light side. But the goal isn't to put in more hours. It's to get more out of the hours you do work.

Now $600 an hour conveniently works out to $10 a minute. So if I may, I would like to ask you to take a $10 bill out of your purse or wallet, put it on the table, and look at it for a minute. At $10 a minute you can see time. At $10 a minute your colleagues and co-workers can see time. At $10 a minute, you don't waste time.

You won't waste your valuable time sitting on hold for several minutes while you're waiting for someone to get off the telephone. You'll leave a message or call back later.

You won't waste 15 to 30 minutes of your valuable time sitting in a reception area as you wait for the person with whom you've scheduled a meeting to complete his current meeting. Instead you'll make it a point to confirm all your meetings and appointments before you leave your office so you can adjust your schedule if others are running a bit late.

And, speaking of meetings, you'll insist that they start on time, end on time, and accomplish the things they were supposed to accomplish. At $10 per minute, multiplied by everybody in the meeting, you just can't afford to waste time. It's too expensive.

Once you begin to realize your time is worth this kind of money, I guarantee you'll start spending it differently. You'll do only the things that are really important. You'll eliminate the things that keep you busy and waste your time. You'll focus your time and energies on the tasks you must accomplish so that you'll achieve your goals.

 SUCCESS TIP

The decisions that come out of meetings can be worth tens of thousands or tens of millions of dollars to your company. They can affect your raises, bonuses, and promotional opportunities. The benefits of a well-run meeting can greatly exceed the cost of $10 per minute for those in attendance.

REMEMBER

- The way you spend your time is a result of the way you see your time and the way you see your priorities.

- Give yourself a raise—in your own mind—increase your level of performance, and you'll travel much faster down the road to success. You'll also make more money than you ever dreamed.

Now, I would like you to take a moment to think about how you spend your 8 to 10 hours during the workday and complete the following chart. What are your five biggest time-wasters? How much time is wasted on each of them every day?

What can you do to eliminate or reduce this drain on your time, energy, and enthusiasm?

BIGGEST TIME-WASTERS	AMOUNT OF TIME WASTED
1. _____	_____
2. _____	_____
3. _____	_____
4. _____	_____
5. _____	_____

Give Yourself an Extra Hour Each Day

When I first started my business career in the early 1970s, Pauline Novak, a woman with whom I worked very closely, planted this thought in my mind:

"If there's something you *really* want to do, get up an hour earlier each morning and work on it *before* you go to work."

Over the years, I've taken this concept to heart. When I've wanted to complete something that was very important to me (this book, for example), I would get up at 5:00 A.M. and work for an hour or longer before eating breakfast.

When you have work that is very important to you, get up early in the morning and give yourself an extra hour of uninterrupted time each day. You're bright and alert, you have lots of energy, your concentration level is high, and most importantly, you're highly motivated. You'll be amazed at how much you're able to accomplish when you focus your energies on completing a single task.

TIMESAVING TIP

Many people spend several hours a day commuting from their homes to their offices. If you're one of them, would it be possible to change your schedule so as to avoid the heavy traffic? This will enable you to convert commuting time into time you can use more productively and effectively. To go one step further, perhaps you can change your work schedule so you could work from home one or two days a week and eliminate the commute altogether.

Do One More Thing Before You Call It a Day

At the end of each day, look at your Master List and do one more task before you call it a day. Make one more phone call. Write one more letter. Find one more thing you can accomplish and cross off your Master List before you go home.

ANECDOTE

The concept of making one more phone call or completing just one more task before calling it a day has helped me further my career in many ways. Since I started doing this I've reached hundreds of people who were still sitting at their desks at 5:30 or 6:00 P.M. And I've completed thousands of tasks that have enabled me to stay at least a couple of steps ahead of my competition.

Think of the impact this has. At the end of your week, you've completed five more items that were on your Master List. At the end of the month, an additional 20 items have been completed. And at the end of the year, you've completed an extra 200 tasks.

REMEMBER

Get more things done during the course of the day, and you'll have more time to chart your course so you can accomplish your goals.

TIMESAVING TIP

Don't put off till tomorrow what can be done now!

Setting Your Priorities

Another thing successful people do is identify and set their priorities. What do I mean by this? You've only got a limited amount of time, a limited amount of money, and a finite amount of energy. If you squander these valuable resources doing things that aren't important and meaningful, you're never going to accomplish the things you're dreaming of. You won't have anything to show for your hard work and effort.

So everything you do must *always* be done with your dreams, goals, and desires in mind. You can't allow yourself to get sidetracked.

SUCCESS TIP

Keep a list of your goals, dreams, and desires taped to your bathroom mirror. Read them out loud when you wake up in the morning and before you go to bed in the evening. Tape another copy of the list on the wall in your office as a constant reminder of what it is you want to do. Every time you start to do a task, ask yourself: "Is this task helping me to achieve my goals?" If it's not, don't do it. If it's a task that *must* be done, do it as quickly and efficiently as possible. Then go back to working on a task that *will* help you to achieve your goals.

Spend your time doing the things that are most important. The things that are of the highest priority. Everything else can wait till later, be delegated to others, or be eliminated.

WHICH TASK IS MOST IMPORTANT?

This is a very simple method you can use to determine which item, task, or project is the most important when you have several important things to choose from. Let's say you have five tasks that need to be done (though this applies to any number of tasks) and you're having difficulty determining which should be done first. Write each of the items on a numbered list.

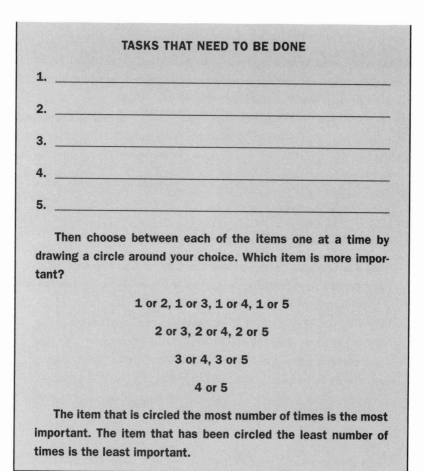

TASKS THAT NEED TO BE DONE

1. _____

2. _____

3. _____

4. _____

5. _____

Then choose between each of the items one at a time by drawing a circle around your choice. Which item is more important?

1 or 2, 1 or 3, 1 or 4, 1 or 5

2 or 3, 2 or 4, 2 or 5

3 or 4, 3 or 5

4 or 5

The item that is circled the most number of times is the most important. The item that has been circled the least number of times is the least important.

Successful People Don't Procrastinate

Successful people aren't procrastinators They don't put things off. They don't spend their time doing the easy things. They don't push their important work, tasks, and projects off until later—which is usually defined as the time when things can't be pushed off any further. They don't wait till the fifty-ninth minute of the eleventh hour to start their projects. They start projects when they're assigned, they do the work properly, and they complete their work on time. Then they move on to the next project.

To succeed in life, you've got to do the hard stuff first. It is for this reason that it's so very important for you to use your Master List to stay on top of everything that needs to be done. By doing so you'll be able to start and complete your work on time.

REMEMBER

- Successful people do the things that need to be done—whether they want to do them or not!

- Procrastination is the biggest career-killer. If you want to be successful you can't put things off because you don't feel like doing them.

HOW DO YOU EAT YOUR CAKE?

I was once asked by a friend: "How do you eat your chocolate cake?" I didn't quite understand the question, so I asked her what she meant. She then asked me this question: "Do you eat the frosting first, or save it to the end?" I said I always eat the frosting first, because it's the best part.

She then asked how I went about doing my work each day. I explained that I always started by doing the work I liked and enjoyed first, and put off the harder tasks for later. Sort of like how I eat my cake.

She suggested I try something different: "Save the good stuff for last." By this she meant that my reward for finishing the hard work—the work I didn't want to do—would be the fun stuff. I've found this to be a very motivating concept. (However, I still eat the icing on my cake first.)

 SUCCESS TIP

Force yourself to work on and complete the hardest, most difficult work first thing in the day, when you're fresh and alert and have lots of energy. Once you've finished you can work on the fun and enjoyable stuff. Another way of saying it: Delay gratification until the hard work's done!

Create a Sense of Urgency by Setting Deadlines

To be successful in any endeavor, you've got to get your work, tasks, and projects done. They need to be done on time, and they need to be done right.

The best way to do this is to create a sense of urgency. With a sense of urgency, you strive to meet your deadlines, you focus your energies, and you make sure the job gets done. This just happens to be one of the best ways you can beat the procrastination habit. Here are some tips:

- **Get Your Work Done Early.** Let's start with the idea of not only meeting your deadlines but beating them. If you're supposed to prepare a report for your boss for a Friday morning meeting, complete the report and deliver it on Wednesday afternoon. One way you can do this is by setting early deadlines so you finish your work before it's due. As a general rule, move up the deadlines for all of your work, tasks, and projects by one or two days. This gives you extra time to think about and review your completed task before it needs to be turned in. It also gives you some extra time—a cushion—so that when things don't go exactly as scheduled, you've still got some time left before the project's due.

- **Give Early Deadlines to Others.** When assigning tasks to others, tell them you need the completed work a day or two earlier than you *really* need it. This gives you a cushion in case there's a delay. It also gives you a bit more time to think before you need to make a decision.

 TIMESAVING TIPS

- When a task is assigned to someone else, always give that person a specific due date and time for completion. Tell him you need the work on your desk by 3:00 P.M. on Wednesday or 9:00 on Thursday morning. This lets the other person know the task is important to you.

- When a task has been assigned to someone else, always call a day or two before the due date to remind the person that you need the task completed by the designated day. This is another reason ACT! is such a powerful time management tool: It helps you become a professional nudge. Remember, the squeaky wheel always gets the grease. Be the squeaky wheel and always stay on top of the work, tasks, and projects that have been delegated to others.

- **Create Deadlines for Tasks That Don't Have Deadlines.** Tasks without deadlines never get done. So assign deadlines to each of your tasks. This way they won't hang around forever. You'll complete them, cross them off your Master List, and go on to your next task.

- **Deliver More Than Is Expected of You.** If you *really* want to make a good impression on your boss, your customers, or anyone else you're supposed to do something for, deliver more than is expected. What do I mean by this? I mean give 110 percent.

- When you're given a goal: Exceed it! When you're given a deadline: Beat it! When you're given the opportunity to perform: Do it!

- Be the person who solves problems.

 REMEMBER

Mistakes cost money. Your goal is to get your work done right the first time.

- Strive to be the best informed, best qualified person in your department, company, or organization.

- Be responsible for the things you do.

DO IT RIGHT!

Whatever you're doing, it's got to be done right! This could be a letter, memo, or report that your boss needs. Or it could be the fulfillment of a multimillion-dollar order.

You must make sure every i is dotted and every t is crossed. This is another reason you should start on your work, tasks, and projects as soon as they're assigned and schedule internal dead-lines that encourage you—and the people with whom you're working—to complete your tasks before your *real* deadlines. It gives you extra time to study and think about the things you've done to see if they were in fact done correctly—and, once they're completed, to look for ways of improving them. Here are some more thoughts:

- *Proofread Your Documents.* When you're writing a letter, memo, report, sales presentation, or anything else, always proofread it. Put it aside for a while and do something else. When you pick it up a second time, study it to see if what you put down on paper was what you really wanted to say.

ANECDOTE

Abe Lincoln once said: "I would have sent a shorter letter, but I didn't have the time." It's easy to write a long letter, or a very lengthy report or presentation, but it takes a lot of work to condense a document to just a few paragraphs or a few short pages.

I've found that I can always improve on something when I give myself the time to think about and proofread it. This is espe-cially true when it comes to spelling and grammatical mistakes. Studies have shown that in most offices, over 85 percent of the papers that cross people's desks have mistakes on them. And the cost of correcting these mistakes can run up to 25 percent of the cost it took to create them in the first place.

You should also study the structure of everything you write. Most people don't have the time to read the things that cross their desks. So always place the most important information—the message you want to convey—in the first sentence of the first paragraph. Tell the reader what you want him to know. The supporting information should follow.

● *Check Your Numbers.* When you're sending out a proposal, or anything else that has numbers on it, double- and triple-check the accuracy of those numbers. Better yet, have someone else study the numbers. Many times others will notice something that's slipped through the cracks because you were too close to it.

ANECDOTE

I once knew of a company that had a multimillion-dollar order to manufacture railroad freight cars. Unfortunately, they priced their order based upon the costs of building a three-sided car. The more cars they produced, the more money they lost. Eventually they were forced into bankruptcy.

Focus on the Important Tasks, Not the Urgent Ones

There's a big difference between doing something that is important and doing something that is urgent. It's very easy for people to find that they spend the majority of their working time doing things that are urgent. We call these people crisis managers. They spend their entire day dealing with crises and emergencies.

By the end of the day, they've spent so much of their time and energy putting out fires that they're exhausted. They have no energy—mental or physical—available for the important tasks and projects they haven't had time to think about. And when these tasks are finally addressed, the lead time has evaporated, another deadline is looming, and everything continues to spiral out of control.

 REMEMBER

When you go through life as a crisis manager, you no longer have control of any of the events in your life.

Often the crises for which we are forced to drop everything are avoidable: Something that should have been done wasn't, or it wasn't done right. Now there's a problem, and you're the one responsible for fixing it.

REMEMBER

Just because it's someone else's emergency doesn't mean it's *your* emergency.

TIMESAVING TIP

As you look at the items you've noted on your Master List, make it a point to *schedule your priorities.* Don't prioritize your schedule. Focus your time and energy on the tasks that are most important.

THE DIFFERENCE BETWEEN BEING *EFFICIENT* AND BEING *EFFECTIVE*

A dictionary defines *efficient* as "performing or functioning in the best possible and least wasteful manner." When you're doing a task you want to complete it in the shortest amount of time and with the least amount of effort.

The word *effective* is defined as "producing the intended or expected result." When you do a task effectively, you're working on the right task at the right time. And you're completing it on time.

Today, many people spend the majority of their time doing tasks efficiently. Unfortunately, they're spending their time doing tasks that aren't important or meaningful.

The successful person tackles his or her important tasks first, does them quickly, and does them right. He is being both *efficient* and *effective.*

Be the Person Who Solves Problems

Life is nothing more than the process of finding ways to overcome a series of problems. The process of meeting and solving these problems is what gives life meaning. It is your ability to overcome—and find solutions to—these problems that will make you a huge success. Here are two points to remember:

- People who don't solve problems never get anything done. Spend your time solving problems, not complaining about them.

- When a problem isn't getting solved, something isn't getting done, and someone isn't happy. That someone could be a customer, a supplier, the boss or supervisor, or a family member. And when people aren't happy they do one of two things: They start complaining, or they vote with their feet and head for the door.

Find a solution to a problem and you grow. You learn something new. Your foundation—your skills, talents, and experience—becomes deeper and wider. You have something more that you can build upon.

 SUCCESS TIP

Become the #1 problem solver and you become *the* expert. Experts make a lot more money than everybody else.

 REMEMBER

You are judged by the quality of the work you produce and the timeliness of that work, not the number of hours you work during the course of a day.

These are the steps you should follow whenever you need to solve a problem:

1. Take the time to analyze and identify the problem.

2. Create a plan of action to solve the problem.

3. Execute your plan.

Once the problem has been resolved, go on to whatever else needs your attention.

Take the Time to Solve Problems

Often, problems don't get solved because the person who is in a position to solve them is just too busy. He or she just doesn't take the time. And what happens to a little problem that doesn't get resolved when it's little? It gets bigger and bigger until it becomes a *real* problem that's going to require a lot of time, energy, and resources to be solved.

It's much easier to confront problems early, while they're still small and manageable. When a problem isn't addressed quickly, it can easily spin out of your control. It's sort of like a forest fire. An ember from a campfire flies onto some dry grass and goes unnoticed. Within the first few minutes this small fire may still be controllable, but in no time at all it's grown beyond the capability of the campers to put it out. It could take hundreds of firefighters many days to extinguish this fire.

What are you really doing when you don't deal with a little problem? You're procrastinating. You're hoping that it'll just go away, or that someone else will take the time to solve it for you.

Unfortunately, problems don't just go away. They must be dealt with, worked through, and brought to a final resolution, or else they remain forever.

 ANECDOTE

Many times I see people walking down the street all hunched over, as if they're carrying the weight of the world on their shoulders. Well, they are. They're carrying the burden of all their problems on their backs and they're getting crushed by the load.

Unresolved problems are a drain on your mental, intellectual, and physical strength. How many times have you heard people say they're "drained"? What they are really saying is that their problems are so voluminous that they've run out of mental and physical energy. They're exhausted, but the problems still remain, and still need to be addressed.

REMEMBER

You don't have to accept responsibility for someone else's problem. But once you accept the responsibility for solving the problem, then it *does* become your problem.

Getting the Most out of Each Day

Each day we start off with the best of intentions. We have important work we want to complete, people with whom we wish to speak, and long-term projects we need to begin working on. But by the end of the day we discover we've only accomplished a fraction of what we wanted. So we're forced to come in early, stay late, and work weekends. Yes, we're busy, but hardly productive.

On the following pages I'm going to give you some time-saving tips, techniques, and strategies that will help you become more productive, get more things done, and maintain control over your day. Utilize these ideas and your journey down on the road to success will be much smoother.

Schedule an Appointment with Yourself

One way to guarantee that you'll get your important, high-priority work done correctly and on time is to schedule an appointment with yourself. The only way you can complete your work is to give yourself uninterrupted blocks of time—30, 60, or 90 minutes—during the course of your day. This enables you to concentrate and focus your attention on the task at hand.

I'm now giving you permission to do the following:

● Close the door (or put up a Do Not Disturb sign across the entrance to your work area).

● Turn off the phone and your beeper, and give yourself some undisturbed quiet time.

● Give yourself some time to think and concentrate as you tackle your important work, tasks, and projects.

If anybody asks you why you're closing the door, turning off the phone, and giving yourself some private time, just tell them time management guru Jeffrey Mayer said it was okay to do so.

Whenever most people have a meeting or a telephone conversation, it probably results in some additional work. I would presume it's the same for you. So the first thing you should *always* do is note the newly assigned task on your Master List or as an activity inside ACT!. This way you won't forget about it. Then you should ask yourself four questions:

1. When does it need to be done?

2. How long will it take?

3. How important is it?

4. When will I do it?

After you've answered these questions, look at your calendar and block out enough time so you can start and complete this task.

TIMESAVING TIP

Most tasks take longer than expected. So give yourself 50 percent more time than you think you'll need.

"BUT I'VE GOT TO BE AVAILABLE FOR MY CUSTOMERS!"

Day after day people tell me they've *always* got to be available for their customers. This is how John's day goes:

John starts to work on a task for Bill. Then the phone rings. It's Sally calling, and she has a question. So John puts Bill's work aside and starts working on Sally's project. Then an express mail package arrives from Fred.

John stops working on Sally's project and begins doing something for Fred. Then the phone rings again and it's Phyllis. She's got a problem, so John drops everything and begins to deal with it immediately.

By the end of the day, John has a number of customers who think their work is being done. But in reality, none of it is. Because of the interruptions, nothing has been completed. Instead, everything is in a state of partial completion. And the long list of unfinished work continues to grow with each passing day. In the end, none of these customers is satisfied.

This is no way to run a business!

Make the Most of Your Prime Time

There's a time of day when we all have lots of energy and enthusiasm. Our ability to think and concentrate is high. This is the time of day when we're capable of doing our best work. I call this Prime Time, the time of day you're at your best.

Some people are good in the morning, others in the afternoon, and there's a third group that do their best work in the middle of the night. Whether you're a morning, afternoon, or middle-of-the-night person, make it a point to use your Prime Time to tackle your most important and demanding tasks.

On the following chart, rate your personal effectiveness at different times during the day. Look at each time period and circle the number that represents your level of productivity. A 5 indicates your most productive time, and a 1 indicates your least productive time.

Use your Prime Time to tackle your most important work, and try your best to schedule your meetings, appointments, and other activities at other times during the day. You'll find you get more done in less time and with less effort.

DAILY EFFICIENCY CHART

		When Do You Do Your Best Work?	
Early Morning	Most	5 - 4 - 3 - 2 - 1	Least
Mid-Morning	Most	5 - 4 - 3 - 2 - 1	Least
Late Morning	Most	5 - 4 - 3 - 2 - 1	Least
Noon	Most	5 - 4 - 3 - 2 - 1	Least
Early Afternoon	Most	5 - 4 - 3 - 2 - 1	Least
Late Afternoon	Most	5 - 4 - 3 - 2 - 1	Least
Early Evening	Most	5 - 4 - 3 - 2 - 1	Least
Middle of the Night	Most	5 - 4 - 3 - 2 - 1	Least

Give Yourself the First Two Hours of the Day

Many years ago I came up with a very simple idea: Combine the two previous time-saving tips.

- Schedule an appointment with yourself.

- Use your prime time to do your most important work.

The majority of people who are working today are morning people. And even if you're not a morning person, you probably hold a job where you're working during the daytime hours, so:

Give yourself the first two hours of the workday.

- *No meetings!*

- *No interruptions!*

- *No telephone calls!*

You'll complete twice the work in half the time with half the effort. This idea alone can make a huge contribution to your achieving success.

Now I know what you're thinking. "I can't go into seclusion for two hours at a time. I've got to be available to answer questions. I've got to be responsive to the needs of my customers, clients, prospects, colleagues, and co-workers, as well as my boss."

But look at this from another perspective. If you don't give yourself some uninterrupted time each day, you'll never complete the work that has already been assigned to you by your customers, clients, prospects, colleagues, co-workers, and boss.

Furthermore, don't you have scheduled meetings with other people throughout the day? Don't you leave the office for lunch? Don't you take telephone calls? You see, you're *really* not available each moment of the work day. Block out some time for yourself during the day and you'll accomplish twice as much in half the time with half the effort.

I know that in the real world it may not be possible to block off two hours of uninterrupted time early in the morning. And depending upon the type of work you do, you may have commitments that take up the early morning hours. But maybe you could give yourself one hour. If you can't do that, then give yourself 30 minutes. The important thing is to give yourself some uninterrupted time during the day so that you can start, and complete, your important work.

 TIMESAVING TIP

Block out time for *you* on your calendar. Open your calendar or appointment book and look at your schedule for the coming month. If you've got any appointments or meetings scheduled for early in the morning, try to reschedule them for later in the day. Now take a red pen or pencil and block out the first two hours of your workday for each day in the month. This will ensure that you've got some private time so you can get to your most important tasks.

REMEMBER

If you wait till the end of the day to begin working on these important tasks, you'll be so worn out and exhausted that you won't be able to produce your best work.

TIMESAVING TIP

Start on your important tasks when they are assigned, and you'll produce higher-quality work. There will be fewer crises and emergencies to deal with, because you will have completed your tasks on time.

Take Control of Your Meetings

Meetings are notorious time-wasters. Most people spend 30 to 50 percent of any given workday in unproductive meetings. In order to make your dreams come true and accomplish the things you want to accomplish in the business of life, you can't afford to waste your valuable and precious time in unproductive meetings.

REMEMBER

An organization in which everybody meets all the time is an organization in which no one gets anything done.

Here are some meeting tips:

- **Don't Have a Meeting:** Just because someone wants to schedule a meeting doesn't mean you have to go. Nor does it mean the meeting must be held. Ask the person why he is calling the meeting and what he wants to accomplish. In most cases the information that would be discussed in a face-to-face meeting can be transmitted over the phone, through the mail, or via e-mail.

- **Have an Agenda:** When you must attend a meeting, insist that an agenda be prepared and distributed in advance. The agenda should list the items for discussion in order of importance, so that everybody knows what is to be discussed. A sample agenda form is included for your use.

- **Someone Must Take Control of the Meeting:** The person who called the meeting has the responsibility to make sure that time isn't wasted discussing unnecessary subjects. He or she must take control of the meeting and keep it moving forward.

- **Meetings Need Starting and Ending Times:** All meetings should have designated starting and ending times. It is up to the person who called the meeting to keep it on time and on track.

REMEMBER

Meetings that start late and run long ruin everybody's day.

- **Meetings Must Have Closure:** At the end of each meeting, conclusions or decisions must be reached. Everybody must know what is expected of him, what will be done next, and the date the work or additional information is due.

REMEMBER

It is unproductive to have a meeting where the only decision made is to schedule another meeting.

TIMESAVING TIP

Always bring your calendar along. If it's necessary to schedule another meeting, a date and time can be selected before everybody walks out the door.

Sample Agenda Form

Date of Meeting _____

Place _____

Starting Time _____

Ending Time _____

Person Calling Meeting _____

Purpose of Meeting _____

Desired Outcome of Meeting _____

Participants

   1. _____

   2. _____

   3. _____

   4. _____

   5. _____

Agenda Items/Time Allotted for Discussion of Each Item

   1. _____

   2. _____

   3. _____

   4. _____

   5. _____

[Note: The most important items should be listed at the top of the agenda and should be discussed first. The person who prepares the agenda should also include the amount of time that will be allowed for discussion of each of these points.]

IDENTIFY THE MOST IMPORTANT ISSUES

Often a number of different issues and/or ideas are brought up during a meeting. Then the group spends an inordinate amount of time trying to determine which of the issues/ideas are the most important. Here is a method you can use to help streamline the determination process:

1. Write the issues/ideas as a numbered list on a flip chart.

2. Have each person write on a piece of paper the numbers of the items he prefers.

3. Record the number of votes each item received.

4. Eliminate the items with the fewest votes.

5. Repeat the process until there are only three items from which to choose.

6. Discuss the remaining items to see if it's possible to reach a consensus based upon the group's goals and/or the problem you are trying to solve.

Avoid Impromptu Meetings

Impromptu meetings, which are really interruptions, are huge time-wasters and productivity destroyers. They break your concentration, disturb your train of thought, and take away your momentum. If you *really* want to take control of your day, you've got to find ways of eliminating these meetings.

Here's an example of a typical impromptu meeting. Someone stops by and asks: "Have you got a minute? I need to talk to you about . . ." Then the person sits down and settles in. Before you know it, 5, 10, 15, 20, 30, or 60 minutes of your day are gone. Yes, the question that was asked only took a moment. Unfortunately the person continued talking about lots of other things and never stopped.

If this only happened once or maybe twice a day it could be OK. But in most offices it happens all day long. (And you wonder why you're putting in so many hours but aren't accomplishing very much.)

REMEMBER

When you allow yourself to be interrupted in this manner you never get anything done.

So the next time a person comes into your office and starts to make himself comfortable, tell him in a firm but friendly tone of voice:

No, I don't have a moment now!
I'm in the middle of a very important task or project.

Then ask the person if you could get together at a mutually convenient time later in the day so you can complete the work, task, or project you're in the midst of. (Of course the person will protest and say, "This will only take a minute." But you've got to be firm.)

When you schedule meetings in this way, you're able to make better use of your time. Now you can bring all the things you need to discuss to the meeting, and the other person can do the same. You've not only eliminated the interruption, you've turned it into an opportunity to have meaningful discussions on a number of other important issues.

Schedule Your Telephone Calls

One of the biggest time-wasters is the telephone. Every time it rings it's an interruption. You stop whatever you're doing to answer the phone, and before you know it you're off in another direction.

I can't stress this enough: It's okay to let a caller leave a message on your voice mail system or your answering machine. It's okay to ask someone to hold your calls for short periods of time.

But if you do choose to pick up the phone, you've also got another choice when you begin speaking to the caller. Just explain to the person that you can't talk at that very moment and, depending upon who the caller is, ask if you could schedule a conference call for later in the day.

Most people think of conference calls as involving three or more people. But I use the term to refer to scheduled telephone appointments. Here are some conference call tips:

- Each party should write down the date and time of the call in his calendar.

- Both parties should take the other's phone number (if they don't have it already) so that each can contact the other if there's a conflict or if one person gets tied up with something else.

- The topic of discussion should be outlined beforehand.

- The parties should determine which one will initiate the call.

Schedule Time to Meet with Your Staff, Colleagues, and Co-workers

Spending time with your staff, colleagues, and co-workers is an important part of most people's day. But in most offices a lot of time is wasted. People are always getting up from their desks to ask someone else a question. This interrupts the other person's day and ends up wasting a lot of everybody's time.

Here are some ideas that will help you solve this problem:

- **Schedule Specific Times to Meet with People.** You may, for example, want to meet with members of your staff late in the morning and once again late in the afternoon. During these meetings you can discuss the issues that have arisen since your last meeting, and others can do the same. This enables you to discuss many issues at once instead of one at a time throughout the day.

- **Have Sales and Staff Meetings Later in the Week.** Most businesses in America hold their sales and staff meetings first thing Monday morning. I feel this approach drains people of their energy and enthusiasm. As an alternative, have the meetings on Thursday or Friday. During these meetings you should go over the specific things you want done the following week. When the staff members arrive on Monday morning, they can sit down at their desks and go to work.

● **Assign Tomorrow's Work This Afternoon.** The best time to assign the tasks that you want a person to work on tomorrow is late in the afternoon today. This gives people time to organize tomorrow's work flow and the opportunity to think about what they need to do. When they arrive in the morning, they can sit down at their desks and go to work.

Taking Control of Your Day

Many people spend 8, 10, or even 12 hours at work each day. Unfortunately, when it's time to go home, they don't feel that they've accomplished very much. Yes, they're busy. Yes, they're working hard. But are they *really* productive? Are they getting results?

These people don't have control over their day, their day has control over them! Here are four techniques you can use to regain control over your day.

Technique #1: Identify Your Three Most Important Tasks

Each day before you go home, look over your Master List and identify the three most important things you *must* complete tomorrow. Write them down on a piece of paper that looks like this:

THE THREE THINGS I WANT TO ACCOMPLISH ON [INSERT DATE]

1. _____

2. _____

3. _____

Then follow these steps:

1. When you arrive in the morning, tackle item #1.

2. When you've completed item #1, start item #2.

3. When you've completed item #2, start item #3.

4. When you've completed item #3, review your Master List and identify the next task you need to tackle.

5. Before you go home, make another list.

Technique #2: Schedule Your Day

Have you ever sat down at the end of the day, created a list of all the things you did during the course of the day, and after reviewing the list decided whether or not you had a productive day?

Many people use this technique. Unfortunately, it doesn't tell you the entire story. It tells you what you did, but it doesn't tell you what you *wanted* to do before the day began.

For many of us, it's far too easy to go through an 8-, 10-, or 12-hour day and discover that though we were very busy, we didn't get to any of the important work, tasks, or projects we had planned to tackle. Yes, we may have gotten a lot of things done, but they may not have been the things we wanted to get done. Or, worse yet, we may not have gotten anything done.

The Daily Agenda Sheet, shown on page 126, is an easy way to find out how well you control your day. It will help you to see how you spend your time during the day, and will give you the answer to the often-asked question: Where Did The Day Go?

This is how you use your Daily Agenda Sheet. Look at your Master List at the end of the day and do the following:

1. Identify the most important task you need to work on tomorrow.

2. Select the time of day you plan to begin working on this task and enter it in the Daily Agenda Sheet's "Things I Plan To Do" column. This should be the first item of business you tackle upon your arrival at the office.

3. Determine how long it will take you to complete this task. Block out that time period.

4. Review your Master List and select the next task you plan to tackle. Select the time you plan to start on this task and block out the time on the Daily Agenda Sheet.

5. Block out your entire day in this manner from start to finish.

REMEMBER

● Most tasks take longer than expected, so give yourself more time than you think you'll need.

● Don't forget to include time for returning phone calls, meeting with customers, clients, and/or people within your organization, and dealing with unexpected emergencies and/or fires.

When you arrive at the office, sit down and go to work. Once you start working, something interesting will happen, the phone will ring, people will walk in with questions, and you'll be interrupted all day long. Your Daily Agenda Sheet is the tool you use to regain control of your day.

This is how you make the power of the Daily Agenda Sheet work for you:

1. Keep the Daily Agenda Sheet on the top of your desk.

2. As the day progresses, enter everything you did, and the time you did it, in the "Things I Did" column.

   • When the phone rings, record who you spoke with and the starting and ending time of the call.

   • When someone walks in and asks a question, write down his name and how much time he took out of your day.

   • When you spend time on a task, record what you did and how long it took you (even if it wasn't a task in the "Things I Plan To Do" list).

At the end of the day you'll have a complete record of everything you did, the time of day you did it, and the length of time it took. Now look at all the things you listed in the "Things I Did" column and compare that list with the tasks you listed in the "Things I Plan To Do" column.

In an instant you'll know whether you controlled your day or it controlled you. Use your Daily Agenda Sheet every day for two weeks, and I can guarantee:

• You'll convert hours of wasted time into productive, meaningful time.

• You'll focus on the tasks that are most important, and complete more work, tasks, and projects than you ever thought possible.

• You'll spend your time doing the things you want to do, not the things other people want you to do.

Daily Agenda Sheet

THINGS I PLAN TO DO		THINGS I DID	
8:00 A.M.		8:00 A.M.	
8:30 A.M.		8:30 A.M.	
9:00 A.M.		9:00 A.M.	
9:30 A.M.		9:30 A.M.	
10:00 A.M.		10:00 A.M.	
10:30 A.M.		10:30 A.M.	
11:00 A.M.		11:00 A.M.	
11:30 A.M.		11:30 A.M.	
12:00 noon		12:00 noon	
12:30 P.M.		12:30 P.M.	
1:00 P.M.		1:00 P.M.	
1:30 P.M.		1:30 P.M.	
2:00 P.M.		2:00 P.M.	
2:30 P.M.		2:30 P.M.	
3:00 P.M.		3:00 P.M.	
3:30 P.M.		3:30 P.M.	
4:00 P.M.		4:00 P.M.	
4:30 P.M.		4:30 P.M.	
5:00 P.M.		5:00 P.M.	
5:30 P.M.		5:30 P.M.	
6:00 P.M.		6:00 P.M.	

WHERE DID THE DAY GO?

Technique #3: Who Are Your Biggest Time-Wasters?

The third technique you can use to regain control over your workday is to keep a daily log of the people who waste the largest amount of your time.

THE FIVE PEOPLE WHO WASTED MY TIME ON [INSERT DATE]

1. _____

2. _____

3. _____

4. _____

5. _____

How much of your time does each of these people waste each day? How do they do it? How do you feel when they leave? What can you do to stop it?

If you allow others to waste your time, you'll never get anything done. You'll be forced to come in early, stay late, and work weekends, and at the end of the day you'll feel tired, worn out, and exhausted. You deserve better.

Technique #4: Keep a Journal of Your Daily Accomplishments

In today's fast-paced world it's too easy to get sidetracked and lose sight of what you want to accomplish. So I would like to suggest that at the end of each day you spend a few moments reflecting upon the things that happened, the things you accomplished, and the things you learned, and make a record of these in a diary or journal. This will help to ensure that you continue moving toward the successful accomplishment of your goals.

 SUCCESS TIP

You can write your journal on a pad of paper, in a spiral notebook, or in a word processing document in your computer.

THE MAJOR THINGS I ACCOMPLISHED ON [INSERT DATE]

1. _____

2. _____

3. _____

4. _____

5. _____

THE THINGS I LEARNED ON [INSERT DATE]

1. _____

2. _____

3. _____

4. _____

5. _____

REMEMBER

When you sit down to analyze the things you did and review the things you accomplished at the end of each day, look at them in comparison with what you wanted to accomplish before you started.

Here is a list of some additional things you may want to think about and record in your journal:

● What did you do right?

● What do you feel good about?

● What could you have done better?

Successful People Build Relationships with the *Right* People

As you go through life, you have two challenges. The first is to find the people with whom you wish to develop long-term relationships. The second is to make these relationships grow, flower, and blossom.

Building and maintaining relationships is one of the keys to being a success in the business of life. Spend your time and energy with the *right* people. People who offer you help, support, and encouragement. People whose friendship and companionship you enjoy. People who want to see you succeed. People who will help you achieve your goals and help you make your dreams come true. People who are your friends.

Every day you are talking with and meeting new people. You're having conversations with colleagues and co-workers, customers, clients, suppliers, and lots of others. Each one of these people represents an opportunity to create a friendship. As you get to know each other better, look for ways in which you can help each other.

 REMEMBER

- Focus on developing, enhancing, and improving your relationships with others. Think of these people as your teammates. When you work together as a team it's easier to solve problems, achieve a common goal, and get results.

- The most important ingredient you put into any relationship is not what you say or do, but who you are. The words and the music must go together.

 ANECDOTE

When Bill Clinton was in college he began keeping track of everybody he met. He kept the names on index cards. From time to time he would call the people or write them letters. He kept detailed records of when he spoke with each of them, when he sent something out, and the response he got. By the time he ran for governor of Arkansas, his card file had grown to include more than 10,000 people. This group of people became known as the Friends of Bill.

As you go through life, your goal should be to expand your network of friends.

Networking: The Art of Making Friends

I'm sure you've been told over and over how important it is to network. But what is networking?

- Networking is the process of searching for people with whom you can develop a relationship.

- Networking is the process of making connections.

- Networking is the process of finding people who can be of help to you (and to whom you can be of help).

- Networking is the process of learning who to call when you've got a problem or when you need to get something done.

ANECDOTE

One day I was flying home from Los Angeles, and I started a conversation with the woman sitting next to me. As we talked, I learned that she had been an attorney in Chicago, had gotten tired of the legal profession, and had decided to move to L.A. Today she's a producer for a very popular television program. When the plane landed we exchanged business cards. I also asked for her home address and phone number. When I got home, I entered her name, address, and phone numbers into ACT!. Then I opened ACT!'s notepad and jotted down a summary of the conversation. Several months later my daughter's school was having a fund-raising benefit. I called the woman I met on the plane and asked if it was possible to get the cast of her show to sign a television script. The script was auctioned off for several thousand dollars. You never know who you're going to meet on an airplane.

Give Yourself the Opportunity to Meet a Lot of People

To network properly you need to give yourself the opportunity to meet a lot of people. But meeting people is only the first step. The second step is devising a system for keeping in touch with each person on a regular basis.

Every day you and I are meeting people:

● We participate in business meetings.

● We attend business conferences and seminars.

● We attend industry meetings.

● We travel on trains, buses, and airplanes.

● We take vacations.

● We stand in line at the grocery store, at the drugstore, at restaurants, at the movies.

● Our kids have school functions and other after-school activities.

Every once in a while we meet someone we would like to get to know better. We may not be sure how such people may be able to help us in the future, or how we can help them, but for some unknown reason we like each other. There's some sort of chemistry between us. This is a chemistry that's worth exploring further to see what happens.

But what do most of us do with these opportunities? We let them slip through our fingers. Why? Because we don't have a systematic way of capitalizing on them.

So if I may, I would like to ask you a question: What do you do when you meet someone? Do you always remember to exchange business cards? If someone doesn't have a card, do you take the time to write his name, address, and phone number on the back of one of yours? And what happens to the card once you return to the office?

● Does it stay in your wallet, purse, or briefcase till the end of time?

● Do you put it in the lap drawer of your desk, where it never again sees the light of day?

● Do you make a Rolodex card, or add the person to your name and address book, and never call the person again?

The end result of all of these is that you lose track of each other.

REMEMBER

The more people you know, the better your connections.

MAKE A GOOD FIRST IMPRESSION

You never have a second chance at making a good first impression. So make sure you come across as someone others will want to connect with. Here are some tips:

- Greet people with enthusiasm.

- Have a bright, heartwarming smile on your face.

- Say "Hi" in a tone of voice that shows people how pleased you are to meet them.

- Shake hands with a strong, firm grip.

REMEMBER

- The expression a person wears on his or her face is far more important than the clothes he is wearing.

- People become more interested in you when you show an interest in them. Put yourself out. Do things for other people that require time, energy, unselfishness, and thoughtfulness.

SUCCESS TIP

A very good book on how to network is Susan Roane's *How to Work a Room* (Warner Books).

YOU'RE NOT GOING TO MAKE FRIENDS WITH EVERYBODY

Early in my business career I was led to believe that every person I spoke with or met should become a friend. But in the real world, or at least the world I was living in, this wasn't the case. I just didn't hit it off with everybody I met, or they didn't hit it off with me. So I stopped trying to become friends with *everybody*.

> Instead, I've pursued the friendships that have appeared to offer the most potential and have worked at nurturing those. Some of these friendships have grown into long-term relationships that go back years or even decades. Other friendships have been short-lived.
>
> The beauty of this approach is that I now have a long list of people whom I like and who like me. And each day I'm working to expand the size of that list.

REMEMBER

The most important thing in business is relationships with people: who you know, how well you know them, and how quickly you can get them on the phone!

Networking with a Paper-Based System

In the old days, before we all had PCs, the key to networking effectively was your Rolodex file, your name and address book (also known as your little black book), or your business card collection. Everybody felt the secret of success was to fill your Rolodex file or name and address book with people's names and information.

- The bigger the better.

- The fatter the better.

- The heavier the better.

Quantity was more important than quality. But these systems didn't really work.

Obese Rolodex Files Aren't Usable

It used to be a status symbol for a person to have several Rolodex files sitting upon his or her desk. This conveyed an image of POWER. It said: "I'm important. I know a lot of people."

Yes, the Rolodex was huge, with hundreds or thousands of names, but in reality only a handful of people were contacted on a regular basis. What happened to the rest? They were lost and forgotten. Why? Because there was no systematic way to schedule automatic follow-ups.

People who are good at meeting other people and collecting business cards will find that their Rolodex files are filled beyond capacity and suffering from obesity in no time at all. So what do they do? They purchase a second or even a third Rolodex file. But this doesn't make the process of staying in touch with people any easier.

Adding New People Is a Cumbersome Process

Adding new Rolodex cards isn't easy. It's a cumbersome—and time-consuming—process. When someone gives you a business card, you do one of three things:

- Retype the information on the business card onto the Rolodex card.

- Rewrite the information by hand onto the Rolodex card.

- Staple the business card to the Rolodex card.

 ANECDOTE

In many offices secretaries and administrative assistants spend hours of valuable time typing Rolodex cards. This is _busy_ work, not _productive_ work. And people wonder why nothing important ever gets done.

And how much information can you _really_ put on those 2×4- or 3×5-inch cards? You can include people's business addresses, phone and fax numbers, and e-mail addresses. But what about a person's home address and phone? Home fax number? Cell phone and car phone numbers? And where do you record the names of someone's spouse and children?

What can you do with the information on the card? Nothing! When you want to write a letter, or address an envelope, how do you get that information onto the piece of paper? You type it. Typing takes time. Wasted time.

Finding People Isn't Easy

Once you've created this enormous card filing system, how do you go about finding the important people in your life? For most of us it isn't easy. Was the person filed under First Name? Last Name? Company? Who remembers?

To make matters worse, there's never any consistency in Rolodex card entries. The first line on some cards may be a company name; on others it's the person's first name; a third group may be entered Last Name, First Name. Some cards may be typed, others handwritten, and still others may consist of business cards stapled to Rolodex cards. Needless to say, it isn't easy to find people in a Rolodex file.

And let's say you're going out of town on a business trip. How do you search your Rolodex file to find everybody you know in Los Angeles, New York, Chicago, or anyplace else?

Or say you're having a special promotion. How do you locate the people who might be interested in your sale on widgets, whatchamacallits, or thingamajigs?

In no time at all the Rolodex file has become an unmanageable nightmare. Yes, there may be hundreds or even thousands of names in it. But it takes forever to find them!

What Happens When a Person Changes Jobs?

Another set of problems arises when a person changes jobs. How do you update the Rolodex card? Most people just scratch out the old information and scribble the new information on the card. Yes, the card has now been updated, but it's probably impossible to read.

And when a person moves on, we scratch his or her name off the card and write in the replacement's name. In most cases the name of the departing person is lost forever because we don't bother to keep track of where he went.

 **SUCCESS TIP**

Keep track of the person who just left, because he probably went to a competing company in the same, or a higher, position. This is how you continue to expand your network of contacts.

Name and Address Books Don't Work Either

Information that's put into a name and address book isn't any more useful than information that's entered on a Rolodex card. Each entry has only a limited number of lines in which you can record the person's name, address, and phone number. And there are only a limited number of lines on a page. When the page is filled, there's no more space.

Once an entry is written on a page, it can't be sorted alphabetically. Names appear on a page in the random order in which they were entered. For example, Azinger could be the first entry on the A page, and Aaron could end up as the last entry.

Furthermore, when entries are made with a pencil, they smudge and become illegible in no time at all. And when they're made with a pen, they can't be erased. And let's not forget that writing these entries by hand can be a time-consuming and laborious task.

 ANECDOTES

- One of my consulting clients has used the same name and address book for well over 10 years. Once all the lines on each page had been used he began to write additional entries around the border of each page. When he showed me his book, many of the entries were illegible; most of the pages were worn from use; and the book had coffee stains all over it. From my point of view, this wasn't a very effective way for him to keep in touch with the important people in his life.

- One day my wife Mitzi and I were at a local park with our daughter DeLaine. As DeLaine was playing, I watched a woman sitting on a nearby bench meticulously rewrite the names and addresses from her old address book into her new one. This certainly wasn't a productive way for her to be using her time.

Business Card Files Just Collect Business Cards

The third way people try to keep business contacts is with a business card file. These are the plastic files into which you insert business cards. Yes, this may be better than just throwing the cards in the lap drawer of your desk. But it's only a way to organize the cards. It doesn't organize the information that's on the cards. From my point of view, this isn't an efficient way to run a business either.

TIMESAVING TIPS

● If you have lots of names in a Rolodex file or have a huge collection of business cards in the lap drawer of your desk, you should consider purchasing a business card scanner. With a business card scanner, you can eliminate the biggest hurdle for getting this important information into your computer—typing it. Seiko Instruments' Smart Business Card Reader is a very good business card scanner. Seiko Instruments, 1130 Ringwood Court, San Jose, CA 95131-1726, phone 800-688-0817. Web site: www .seikosmart.com.

● If you've got mailing lists, business cards, or Rolodex files that you would like to have typed into your computer, call Contact Data Entry. Send them your lists, and they'll type the names into their computer and send them back to you. Within minutes, you'll have your list of names inside your computer. Contact Data Entry, P.O. Box 3998, Bartlesville, OK 74006, phone 918-335-0252. Web site: www.contactentry.com.

To say the least, paper-based systems are cumbersome. It isn't easy to locate names, addresses, and phone numbers. There's only limited space available on a card or in an address book. And because the information is on paper, the only way you can use it—when you need to send a letter, for example—is by retyping it. A huge waste of time.

You'll be much better served by putting your Rolodex file and/or name and address book into your computer, which just happens to be what I cover next.

Put Your Name and Address Book Inside Your Computer

I don't believe it's possible to network effectively using a paper-based system—a Rolodex file, a name and address book, or a business card collection. There are just too many limitations. You can't find people quickly. You have no place to store fax numbers, mobile phone numbers, car phone numbers, e-mail addresses, Web site addresses, or any other types of addresses. And most importantly, there's no place to store information about people.

The Way I Used to Do It

When I started my business career in the early 1970s, I was taught to keep detailed information about everybody with whom I spoke. This included the correct spelling of the person's name, his complete mailing address and phone number(s), and lots more.

In addition, I kept notes of every telephone conversation and face-to-face meeting, and I maintained a record of everything that was sent to or received from each person. These notations were made on sheets of paper called Case History sheets. Each person's Case History sheet was kept in his or her manila file folder.

With this system I no longer needed to rely on my memory. Whenever I spoke with a person I always pulled out his file for reference. It took just a few moments to review the Case History sheet—where I had a complete record of everything that had transpired between us—and I was ready to talk business.

And when I spoke with a new person, my assistant created a new file folder with a typed gummed label. The Case History sheet and any other papers, documents, or records were placed in the folder, which was then placed in a file drawer.

To keep track of everything that needed to be done, a very elaborate tickler system was created. This paper-based system gave me a lot of control, and I had a great deal of information at my fingertips. (At one point my filing system took up almost 10 file drawers and contained several thousand manila folders!)

But I moved a lot of paper back and forth—files needed to be pulled from the file drawers every morning and replaced at the end of the day. Yes, the system worked, but it was cumbersome, time consuming, and expensive. And it took a lot of work to maintain.

Then I discovered ACT!. It changed my life. It worked the way I did. These are the things ACT! did for me:

- ACT! enabled me to take all of the information I had kept so meticulously in my manila folders and put it into my computer.

- ACT! gave me an electronic place to put the names, addresses, and phone numbers of all the people in both my business and personal life.

- ACT! enabled me to use my computer to keep track of my daily activities—calls, meetings, and things to-do—electronically instead of manually.

- ACT! gave me a place where I could keep detailed notes on each of my meetings or telephone conversations.

Once I started using ACT! I said good-bye to my manila files. I got rid of my obese Rolodex file. The name and address book went, and so did the collection of business cards.

ACT! Is the Ultimate Networking Tool

It's my personal belief that everybody should be using ACT!. ACT! is easy to use and is a great time-saving tool. It enables you to automate many of the tasks you are presently doing manually with a pencil and a piece of paper. This helps you to save time, get more things done with less effort, be more productive, and make more money. (In case you've forgotten, I discussed how to automate your follow-up system with ACT! in Success Step 3. If you haven't read that part of the book, I suggest that you take a few minutes and read it now. Then come back to this section.) These are some of the things ACT! can do for you.

An Electronic Name and Address File

Everything in life revolves around people. And ACT! enables you to keep in touch with thousands of people easily and effortlessly. Furthermore, it gives you a place to store a huge amount of information about the important people in your life.

You start by entering a person's work and home addresses, phone and fax numbers, and e-mail and Web site addresses. You can also enter personal/family information. This could include the names of the person's spouse and children, birth dates and anniversaries, outside interests and hobbies, and so on. ACT! is so flexible, you can use it to store almost anything that's important to you.

ACT! can also be used to keep track of specific business information. This could include such things as:

- The date of the last sale

- The amount of the sale

- Products or services the person might be interested in purchasing at a future time

- Contract expiration dates

- Current suppliers and/or vendors

With this information you have the opportunity to get to know each of the important people in your life better. With the passage of time you'll become friends.

The ACT! Contact window is shown in Fig. 5.1.

It's Easy to Find People in ACT!

Once you've added people to your ACT! database, it's easy to find them. You can locate anybody in your database by First Name, Last Name, Company, City, State, ZIP code, or almost any other search criteria that might come to mind. You can assign people to categories such as customer, client, prospect, attorney, banker, accountant, friend, family, or any other classification that would be appropriate to your business, and find the people within each category in the blink of an eye.

 ANECDOTES

- I do all of my own publicity and run my own public relations firm from within ACT!. Over the years I've been interviewed by hundreds of magazine writers, newspaper reporters, radio talk show hosts, and television producers. Every time I speak with someone

```
ACT! - [Act4_demo - Contacts]                                    _ □ x
 File   Edit   Contact   Lookup   Write   Reports   Tools   View   Window   Help         _ & x

 |◄  ◄    17 of 36    ►  ►|

 Company    Mayer Enterprises              Address    50 East Bellevue Place
 Contact    Jeffrey Mayer
 Title      President
 Department                               City       Chicago
 Phone      312-944-4184      Ext          State      IL
 Fax        312-944-4184                   ZIP Code   60611
 Salutation Jeffrey                        E-mail Address  jeff@actnews.com
 ID/Status  Customer                       Web Site   www.ACTnews.com
 Last Results Just received information

 User 1                                    User 7
 User 2
 User 3                                    User 8
 User 4
 User 5                                    User 9
 User 6

 Alt Phone         Ext                     Home Address 1
 Car Phone                                 Home Address 2
 Pager                                     Home City
 Home Phone                                Home State         Home Zip
                                           Home Country

 ◄ ► Notes/History  Activities  Groups  User Fields  Phone/Home  Alt Contacts  Status

 Lookup: All Contacts          Jeff's 4.0 Layout  ▲    <No Group>  ▲
```

Figure 5.1   The ACT! Contact window.

I always add that person to my ACT! database. Today, my list of media contacts has grown to more than 2000 people. With a few clicks of my mouse I can find anybody who works for a magazine in New York City, or anybody who writes for a newspaper in Los Angeles. Try doing this with your Rolodex file.

● One day I was trying to find a certain newspaper reporter in Dallas. But I couldn't remember his name. So I did a search of Dallas, and I came up empty. Then I did a search of Texas, and there he was, in Fort Worth.

 SUCCESS TIP

The next time you go on a business trip, search your ACT! database for the names of all the people you know in that specific town. This way you can schedule multiple appointments and make better use of your time. You can also use ACT! to store the names of your favorite restaurants and hotels.

Everybody's Got a Notepad

In ACT! everybody has his own notepad. Notepads are under the Notes/History tab shown in Fig. 5.2. As I just mentioned, I was trained to keep notes of what transpired in every meeting I attended and every telephone conversation I had. ACT! makes this easy to do because everybody has his own notepad.

SUCCESS TIP

Each time you speak with someone, just open the notepad and jot down a summary of the conversation.

Once you get into the habit of recording notations of your meetings and phone conversations you'll find your productivity improves dramatically. You'll have a huge amount of information at your fingertips, and you will no longer need to write anything down on little pieces of paper or commit it to memory.

SUCCESS TIPS

● The more you write down, the less you have to remember, and the more control you have over your day.

● Look for people who are going to say YES. The notepad is a great way to determine where your relationship with a person is going. Keep detailed notes, and you can see how many times you spoke with people who said they wanted to do business with you but never placed the order, or how many times you left a message but never got called back. Over time you'll have a long list of these

Date	Type	Regarding
1/20/99	Note	We talked about the new long-term contract
1/20/99	Letter Sent	ACT! 4 for Windows for Dummies book
1/10/99	Call Received	Request copy of ACT! in ACTion newsletter - Newsletter mailed
12/20/98	To-do Done	Send copy of Success is a Journey
11/15/98	Letter Sent	ACT! 4 for Windows for Dummies sent
8/28/98	Call Completed	Follow up on meeting - System was purchased. Will be installed in 2 weeks
8/18/98	Meeting Held	Discussed Purchase of new computer system

Figure 5.2   ACT!'s Notes/History tab.

people's reasons and excuses for not saying YES. Get rid of these people and look for better prospects.

● When you're speaking with someone, and he offers an interesting piece of personal information—he is going on vacation to celebrate a birthday or anniversary, or a family member is ill—always enter it into the notepad. When you next speak with the person you can ask how the vacation went or how the relative is feeling. And when people mention the names of other people within their organization, always jot down the colleagues' names. At some future time you can ask to be introduced.

 ANECDOTE

One day I received a call from the assistant of Sally, one of my clients. The assistant informed me that Sally wouldn't be able to keep her appointment because her daughter had become ill. When we got together a few weeks later, the first thing I asked Sally was how her daughter, Cheryl, was doing. She was very surprised that I even knew about her daughter's medical problem and pleased that I had inquired about her health. I would also like to mention that I got the order.

ACT! Makes It Easy for You to Communicate with People

From my perspective, names, addresses, and phone numbers that are on paper are worthless. You can't do anything with them. Put them inside ACT!, however, and you have a license to print money. Here's a list of some of the things you can do easily and effortlessly from within ACT!. These features will help you save lots of time, and will make you much more efficient and effective.

● **Write Letters:** When you need to write a letter, just click the letter icon and ACT! automatically inserts the recipient's name and address into a form letter template in the word processor of your choice—Word, WordPerfect, or ACT!'s own word processor. The days of retyping name and address information are over.

SUCCESS TIPS

- Create form letter templates for frequently sent letters. This will save you time and make you much more productive.

- If you send a lot of letters you *must* get yourself a copy of DAZ-zle. DAZ-zle is a software program, made by Envelope Manager Software, that makes printing envelopes or labels a breeze. Envelope Manager's phone number is 800-576-3279, and you can visit their Web site at www.envelopemanager.com.

- **Perform Mail Merges:** Have you ever wanted to send a form letter to a small or large group of people? It's easy to do in ACT!. Just select the people to whom you wish to send the letter, select the form letter you want to use, and ACT! executes the mail merge. The letters can then be printed, sent as faxes, or sent as e-mail. No muss, no fuss.

- **Send Faxes:** Once you've created your letter it can be sent out as a fax without ever being printed on a piece of paper. ACT! has complete integration with WinFax PRO, the leading faxing software. To get more information about WinFax PRO, you can call Symantec customer service at 800-441-7234 or visit their Web site at www.symantec.com/winfax.

- **Send and Receive E-mail:** ACT! can be used to send and receive all your e-mail. When an e-mail message is sent from ACT!, the message's subject line is recorded as an entry in the recipient's History file. With this feature you have a complete record of each e-mail message you've sent.

- **Keep Telephone Numbers at Your Fingertips:** Click the Phone icon, and a list of all of a specific person's phone and fax numbers is displayed. This is shown in Fig. 5.3. If your computer and telephone share the same phone line, ACT! dials the phone for you. I've found this feature to be a huge time-saver.

- **Attach Files to Contacts:** Once you've created a letter, document, fax, e-mail message, presentation, spreadsheet, scanned image, or anything else, it can be attached to an ACT! contact record. Click on the attachment icon and ACT! opens the attached file.

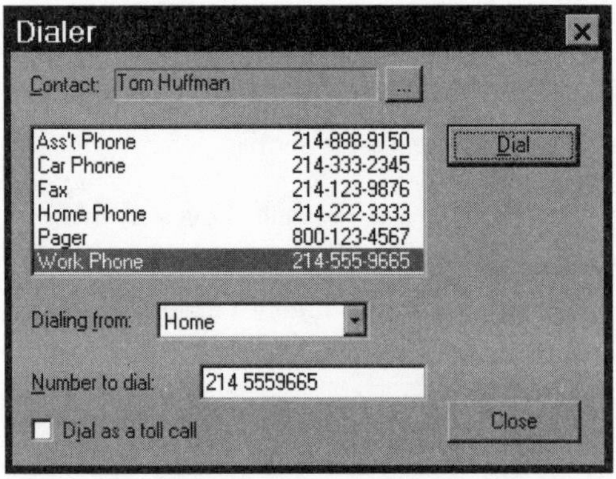

Figure 5.3   Phone List dialog box.

- **Surf the Internet:** Click on a customer's Web site in ACT!'s Web site field and ACT! launches your Web browser and takes you to the selected site. You can also add your favorite Web sites to ACT!'s pull-down menu.

- **Use the History File:** ACT!'s History file provides a place to automatically record all the things that have gone on between you and every person in your ACT! database. For example, you can keep track of the number of times you called a person and left a message, then make another notation of whether that person did in fact call you back. You've also got a record of each letter, fax, and/or e-mail message that was sent. The Record History dialog box is shown in Fig. 5.4.

Getting the Most out of ACT!

Now that you know a little bit about what ACT! does, this is how you can use ACT! to take control over your day:

- **Put Everybody into ACT!.** Whenever you speak with someone, *always* enter his name into ACT!. This enables you to have an electronic Rolodex file. In the blink of an eye you can find anybody in the database.

- **Always Record Your Notes.** Whenever you speak with a person, *always* record a note of the conversation. This way you have a

Contact:	Bouffard, Mitzi [Bouffard Design] ▼

New Contact...

Date: 1/21/99 ▼

Time: 10:20PM ▼

Activity type: Call ▼

Regarding: Wants a copy of Success is a Journey ▼

Result: ⦿ Completed   ○ Received call
        ○ Attempted   ○ Left message

Follow Up Activity...   OK   Cancel

Figure 5.4   ACT!'s Record History dialog box.

record of who said what and when. Best of all, you won't have to deal with little scraps of paper anymore.

- **Schedule Your Activities.** Almost every time you speak with someone, it generates some type of follow-up activity. When you have to do something—write a letter, produce a report, work on a project, and so on—schedule a to-do item. When someone else is supposed to do something, *always* schedule a follow-up call to make sure the task gets done when it is supposed to.

 ANECDOTE

On any given day my list of things to-do or people to call has more than 100 items. My goal is not to get everything on the list completed each day. My goal is to get the important items completed. I'll deal with the remaining items at some future time. I just don't want to forget about them.

Throughout the day, look at ACT!'s Task List and select the task that you must do next. Then block out some time, do the task, and select your next task. The Task List is shown in Fig. 5.5.

- **Communicate with People.** When you need to send a letter, just click the Letter icon and ACT! puts the recipient's name in the

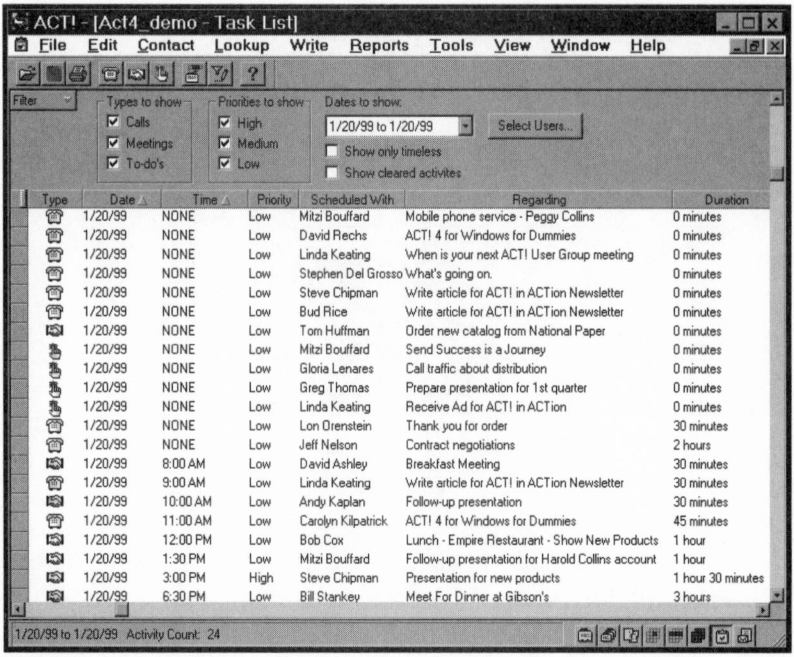

Figure 5.5 ACT!'s Task List.

form letter template. Then write the letter and print it out, or send it as a fax or e-mail. This enables you to stay in touch with people easily and effortlessly.

Launch ACT! the moment you arrive at work in the morning, and don't turn it off until you call it quits for the day. By my own estimation, ACT! enables me to do the work of four or five people all by myself, easily and effortlessly. It should be able to do the same for you.

STEP 6

Successful People Get to Know the Important People in Their Lives

Now that we've discussed the importance of enhancing relationships with people, let's put this to practical use. In Step 6 you're going to learn the *art of networking*. You start by getting to know the important people in your life. Then you expand your circle by getting to know the friends of the important people in your life. Think of *networking* as the art of making and keeping friends.

The Art of Networking

Now I would like you to take a few moments and think of all the people you know. Now make a list of the ten most important people in your life. This can include personal contacts, business contacts, and family members.

THE TEN MOST IMPORTANT PEOPLE IN MY LIFE

1. _____

2. _____

3. _____

4. _____

5. _____

6. _____

7. _____

8. _____

9. _____

10. _____

Since these people are so important to you, it would be a good idea for you to get together with or stay in touch with each of them on a regular basis. So pick up the phone and ask them to join you for breakfast, lunch, dinner, or a cup of coffee, and give yourself the opportunity to enhance and improve your relationships.

How frequently should you have contact with each of these people? Daily? Weekly? Biweekly? Monthly? Once every few months? Whatever you think is appropriate. Schedule a follow-up call as a reminder to get together.

Now I would like you to make another list. This one is a list of the people you would like to get to know better.

TEN PEOPLE I WOULD LIKE TO GET TO KNOW BETTER

1. _____

2. _____

3. _____

4. _____

5. _____

6. _____

7. _____

8. _____

9. _____

10. _____

ALWAYS SCHEDULE AN ACTIVITY

We all have people with whom we want to keep in touch on a regular basis. So you should *always* schedule a follow-up call—even if it's 3, 6, or 12 months in the future—to ensure that you'll keep in touch with the important people in your life.

With ACT!'s recurring activity feature you can schedule a follow-up activity—a call, meeting, or thing to do—for any frequency that's appropriate: daily, weekly, monthly, or annually. This way you'll never forget to maintain regular contact with the important people in your life.

ANECDOTE

One day I was working with John. During our meeting he mentioned that the previous year he had forgotten to invite

> one of his best customers to play golf. To ensure that this oversight didn't happen again, we scheduled an ACT! activity to remind John to call his friend the first of every May and schedule a golfing date.

Now pick up the phone and set up a date for breakfast, lunch, dinner or some other activity where you can get to know each of these people better.

Now let's take a moment to think about the 20 people you just included on your lists. What are the qualities and characteristics that you find so attractive about these people? What are the ties that bind your friendship together? What are the common traits you share with each person? Let's note these on the following list.

COMMON QUALITIES AND CHARACTERISTICS

1. _____

2. _____

3. _____

4. _____

5. _____

6. _____

7. _____

8. _____

9. _____

10. _____

Now that you've identified the qualities and characteristics of the people with whom you want to spend your time, your challenge is to find more people who have the same qualities and characteristics as those on your list.

Get to Know the Friends of the Important People in Your Life

Successful people know successful people. And each person on your lists knows many other people. So as you get to know a person better, ask to be introduced to the important people in his life. When you meet these people you'll probably discover that you have much in common.

Getting an Introduction

During your conversations with friends and relatives, colleagues and co-workers, customers, clients, and prospects, and everyone else you meet, people will always mention the names of other people they know. This could be colleagues at work, people they know through business, or their personal friends. When they mention the name of someone you would like to meet, encourage them to tell you a bit more about that person and ask if they would be so kind as to introduce the two of you.

Or, if you don't think it's appropriate to ask for an introduction at that particular moment, make a mental note about the person. When you return to your office, write down the person's name in ACT!'s notepad. If you can't remember the name, write down something descriptive about the person so you can ask for an introduction at some future time.

The next time you meet with or speak to your friend, bring along the names of the people that he or she had previously mentioned, and ask if he would be kind enough to introduce you. You could say something like: "Sally, when we had lunch recently you mentioned that Bill Smith is a good friend of yours. It sounds like he's doing some very interesting things. Would it be possible for the three of us to meet for lunch sometime? I would like the privilege of meeting him."

THE IMPORTANCE OF REMEMBERING A PERSON'S NAME

The name a person is most interested in hearing is his own. So when you meet another person and remember his or her name, you pay him a very high compliment. You make the person feel important.

When you meet someone for the first time, take the time and energy to learn and remember his name. Here are some techniques you can use to help you remember a person's name:

- Repeat the name to yourself two or three times so as to fix it indelibly in your mind.

- Ask the person to tell you the proper spelling of his name. For example, you could ask: "Kathy, is your name spelled with a K or a C? And what is the proper spelling of your last name?"

- Once the person spells the name for you, repeat the spelling out loud. While you're spelling, look at the person's face and try to make a direct association between name and face in your mind's eye.

- Try to think of something that rhymes with the person's name.

And don't forget to smile as you say something complimentary about the person's name, such as: "That's a very pretty name," or "That's the name of my [son/daughter/mother/best friend]."

The Art of Keeping in Touch

Whenever you meet someone with whom you would like to keep in touch, you should *always* do the following:

1. Take his business card. If the person doesn't have one, write his name, address, and phone number on the back of one of yours. If you don't have a business card, write the information on a piece of paper or a napkin.

2. When you get back to your office, immediately enter the information into ACT!.

3. Write a note to yourself in the notepad as a summary of what you know about the person.

4. Schedule a call for sometime in the near future so you can get together with the person to talk about business opportunities or whatever else may be appropriate.

Networking Is a Lifelong Process

Networking is a lifelong process. It is something you do every day. When you meet someone or hear of a person who sounds interesting, pounce on the opportunity to get to know him better.

As I've said throughout this book, the name of the game is who you know, how well you know them, and how quickly you can get them on the phone. Through meeting new people you expand your network of contacts, you expand your opportunities, and you find a group of people who want to help you achieve your goals and make your dreams come true. You have something to offer them; they have something to offer you. It's called friendship.

Look for People with Whom You've Got Chemistry

You're not going to hit it off with everybody you meet, so don't worry about it. Yes, a person may appear to meet a certain criterion that you've created, but for some unknown reason the two of you don't click. There's such a thing as chemistry, and sometimes you've got it, other times you don't.

This is another way ACT!'s notepad helps you to enhance your relationships. It gives you a place to record your thoughts, comments, and/or opinions about how your relationships with other people are developing.

With some people you'll see that things are going great, and you'll grow closer. With others you'll see red flags that indicate something isn't right. Don't ignore those red flags, just be prepared to move on.

Don't waste your precious time and energy pursuing dead-end relationships. Instead work at strengthening your close relationships.

Your challenge in life is to surround yourself with people with whom you've got chemistry, and minimize your involvement with those with whom you don't. Spend your time and energy searching for people who want to become your friends.

Your goal in life is to surround yourself with people whom you like, and who like you. Follow this process for the rest of your life and you'll have a huge network of friends. You and they together will accomplish more than any of you ever dreamed.

Networking Within Your Own Organization

How well do you know the people with whom you work? What do you know about their dreams, goals, and desires? And what do they know about you?

Many of the people with whom you work can help you become successful. But you've got to work at developing relationships with them.

Get to Know Your Boss Better

No matter where you work, or who you work for, you've got to answer to somebody. Everybody's got a boss or supervisor. Even if you're the owner of your own business, you've got to keep your customers happy, you've got to have a good working relationship with your suppliers, and you've got to have a close relationship with your bankers, lenders, investors, and employees.

However, most of us answer to somebody, and the better your working relationship with your boss or immediate supervisor, the easier it will be for you to get ahead in life. You'll enhance your career opportunities, and your probability of being successful in your chosen business or profession will be greatly increased.

So let me ask you a few questions: How much do you know about your boss?

- What did he or she do before taking his or her current position?

- What other businesses or industries has he or she worked in?

- Where did he or she go to school?

- What do you know about his or her personal life? Single, married, or divorced? Spouse's age? Birthday? Spouse's name? Does the spouse work? Anniversary? Names of kids?

- What are his or her outside interests?

- What are the most important things in his or her life?

- What are his or her goals, dreams, and ambitions?

- What can you do to further his or her career?

Would you like to have a long-term relationship with this person? A relationship that would extend beyond your current position and employment? Many times people's careers are intertwined. When the boss leaves for a better job, some of his staff and co-workers join him at the new company. Do you feel that this is the kind of relationship you would like to have with your boss? If so, help your boss solve his problems, and as his career blossoms, you'll go along for the ride.

Get to Know the Important People Within Your Company or Organization

Within every organization there are people who are movers and shakers. There are people who are the decision makers. There are people who hold the purse strings and control the flow of money.

These are people who, like yourself, are going places. Get to know them better. Make friends with them. Do everything you can to help them accomplish their dreams, goals, and desires, and they'll help you accomplish yours.

REMEMBER

The more people you know within an organization, and the more you know about them, the more your position within the organization is enhanced.

And what about the people with whom you speak on the phone? These could be your customers or your suppliers. Which of these people do you think will be going places? Get to know them better.

Make a list of at least five people within your own company or organization that you would like to get to know better. Now call them up and schedule a date for breakfast, lunch, or coffee. And make it a point to keep in contact with them on a regular basis.

**FIVE COLLEAGUES OR CO-WORKERS I WOULD LIKE
TO GET TO KNOW BETTER**

1. _____

2. _____

3. _____

4. _____

5. _____

Get to Know the Important People Within Your Business or Industry

In addition to getting to know the most important people within your company, get to know, and become friends with, the movers and shakers within your business or industry. Attend industry conferences and seminars. Join—and become an active member in—the local and/or national chapters of your professional association(s). Volunteer to serve on committees. Become an officer.

Make a list of five important people within your business or industry that you would like to get to know better within the next 12 months. Now pick up the phone and set up a date to get together.

**FIVE PEOPLE WITHIN MY INDUSTRY I WOULD LIKE
TO GET TO KNOW BETTER**

1. _____

2. _____

3. _____

4. _____

5. _____

 **SUCCESS TIP**

You can also learn about the movers and shakers, and the up-and-comers, by reading your industry trade journals.

Who Are Your Most Profitable Customers?

The next section focuses on people who are in sales. But even if you aren't in that field, you should still read this because I'm going to give you a very interesting perspective on how to make your business grow.

To make it big in business, it's not necessary to have lots of sales, it's just necessary to close the *right* sales. There's an old saying, one you've probably heard many times over the years: "Eighty percent of your business comes from 20 percent of your customers."

Well, if that's the case, here's something else to think about: Why bother with the remaining 80 percent of your customers who generate only 20 percent of your business?

Now I'm not suggesting you get rid of *everybody* else. But I want to encourage you to think about who, or what, makes a good—and profitable—customer.

When You Have a Lot of Customers, You Have a Feeling of Security . . . False Security

There's a feeling of security that comes with having a lot of customers, or prospective customers, even when they aren't good ones. Yes, you do have a feeling of security. But it's *false* security.

Though you may have many customers, only a small number could really be considered great customers. Another group would be considered good customers. And then there's the rest. These are the people who take up too much of your time, energy, knowledge, and expertise and don't do enough business with you to justify the investment you're putting into them.

That's why I asked the question, "Who are your most profitable customers?" From my perspective, a profitable customer is one who pays his or her bills on time and doesn't demand that you provide a great deal of additional time and attention.

On the other hand, just because a customer spends a lot of money with you doesn't mean that that account is profitable. If it's necessary to provide the customer with an inordinate amount of daily service and maintenance, this extra attention is eating up your profit margin.

So this is what I suggest you do: Clean house and get rid of your unprofitable customers—the ones that take up a lot of your time and energy—and you'll have two huge benefits:

1. You can spend more time working to keep your profitable customers happy.

2. You can spend your time searching for even better customers who match the profile of your most profitable customers.

This is yet another way ACT! and its notepad make you more successful. You have the ability to keep an ongoing record of every meeting and telephone conversation with each person, and a summary of every letter, fax, or e-mail message sent. This information tells you how much time, effort, and energy you're putting into each customer. You can then weigh that against the profit you're making on each customer's business. These are some of the things ACT! can help you can keep track of:

- How many times the person calls with a question that takes up your valuable time but doesn't result in any revenue.

- The amount of time and resources expended as you research the answer to the customer's question(s).

- The number of times a person asks you to put together a bid or quotation, but doesn't place an order with you.

- The number of times you reach people on the phone and they say they're too busy to talk and ask you to call back another time.

- The number of times you call and leave a message without ever receiving a return call.

REMEMBER

When you're spending your time on unprofitable customers, you're being kept from working on other business opportunities or servicing the needs of your profitable customers.

Make a list of your 10 most profitable customers. Take a moment to look at each name on the list and ask yourself these questions:

- How much time during the day or week do you spend making sure that all of their needs, wants, and desires are being satisfied?

- Is there anything more you can do to satisfy their needs?

- If you had more time, what more could you do for each of them?

In addition to your primary contact at each of these companies, how well do you know the other people within the organization? The person's colleagues and co-workers? His or her boss, supervisor, and/ or direct reports?

MY TEN MOST PROFITABLE CUSTOMERS

1._____

2._____

3._____

4._____

5._____

6._____

7._____

8._____

9._____

10._____

In today's fast-paced and highly competitive business world, people are here today and gone tomorrow, so it's important to know everybody within an organization. What are you going to do when your primary contact (and close friend) at your biggest and most profitable account leaves and you don't know a thing about the person who is replacing him?

SUCCESS TIP

Build relationships with *all* the key people within an organization.

It's my suggestion that you get to know the person's assistant, his direct reports, and the people he reports to. If you can get to know the president of the company, or the head of the division, you'll be in a much better position to weather the storm if there's a personnel shakeup.

SUCCESS TIPS

- Once you've met people, start accumulating information about them. The more you know about them, the closer your relationship becomes.

- Ray Considine and Ted Cohn have written a wonderful book on how to improve your customer service and make it easier for your customers to do business with you. It's called *WAYMISH: Why Are You Making It So Hard for me to give you my money?* You can reach Ray at 888-*WAYMISH* (888-929-6474) or 626-795-4282. He's located at 3452 East Foothill Boulevard, Pasadena, California 91107. His e-mail address is raycon1@rayconsidine.com.

Getting to Know People

Throughout this Success Step we've discussed *who* you should get to know better. In this section of Success Step 6, I explain the kind of information you should try to gather.

SUCCESS TIP

It's easy to get this information. All you've got to do is ask questions and listen to the answers . . . which just happens to be discussed in the next Success Step.

I do want to mention that you don't have to gather this information in one sitting. And I'm not suggesting that you try to do so. You glean a little bit at a time over a period of months, years, and decades.

For some people, you will end up knowing almost everything that is going on in their lives. For others, you'll know very little. Some people you'll become very close to, and other people will be little more than acquaintances.

This is one of the beauties of using ACT!. It provides a place for you to record information about everybody you know. Once this information is in the database, it's always at your fingertips.

As you talk to people and get to know them better, always keep these thoughts in the back of your mind:

- What are their goals, dreams, and desires?

- Where have they been?

- Where do they want to go?

- How can you help?

This is the kind of information you should learn about the important people in your life.

Basic Information

Whenever you meet a person, you should try to get the following basic information:

- The correct spelling of the person's name; the company name; mailing address; phone and fax numbers; e-mail address and Web site if appropriate.

 **SUCCESS TIP**

Always ask if a middle name or initial is used.

- The person's preferred form of address—Is a nickname used? What salutation should appear on letters or other correspondence?

- The name and phone number of the person's assistant(s).

Business or Professional Information

In addition to the personal information, ask about the person's business or profession. These are the types of questions you should be asking:

- What type of business is the person in?

- What is the person's position or title and job responsibilities?

- Where does the person fit into the organizational structure? Who is the person's boss or supervisor? Who are his or her colleagues and/or subordinates?

- Who are the decision makers within the organization?

- Who are the person's previous employers?

- What are the person's previous careers or professions?

- What is the person's educational background? Special awards? Is he or she active in alumni associations?

- Are there any outside business interests or affiliations? Is the person a member of any clubs? Industry organizations or trade groups?

- Is there any additional information that could be useful to you based upon your specific business or industry?

Personal Information

You would like to learn the following personal information:

- The person's age and birthday.

- Family status: single, married, divorced, widowed?

- If the person is married, what is the spouse's name? The spouse's birthday? Their anniversary? What kind of work does the spouse do?

- If the person has children, what are their names? Ages? Year in school? Are they doing anything noteworthy?

- Information on the person's parents, brothers, and sisters.

Outside Interests

What kinds of things does the person do when he or she isn't working?

- What does the person do in his or her free time?

- Are there any hobbies or outside interests?

- What are the person's political thoughts and opinions?

SUCCESS TIP

Sometimes it's best to leave political comments and/or discussions out of a friendship.

Goals, Dreams, and Desires

What does this person dream of doing with his or her life? What are his financial goals? Career goals? Family goals?

How can you help make these dreams come true?

Spend Your Life Making Friends

As you go through life, give yourself the opportunity to become friends with the people you meet. You're in a position to help make their dreams come true, and they can do the same for you. You just never know when you'll meet somebody who could change your life.

STEP 7

Successful People Strive for Excellence

To get what you want in life, you need to work in a cooperative way with other people. Make friends with them. Work hard to win them over to your way of thinking. Convince each one that by working together you can accomplish much more than you could going it alone.

This is called *synergy.* The sum of the parts is greater than the whole. Blend and combine the skills, talents, education, training, and strengths of individuals into a single entity, and you've created an organization, a team.

 REMEMBER

Through teamwork you'll accomplish much more than if you try to do the same things alone. Life is easier when you're *all* pulling in the same direction.

There Is No I in Team

When you become a team member, I becomes We. As a team member you give up a small part of yourself so the team as a whole can grow and prosper.

Open up the possibilities for people to strive to achieve their performance objectives and grow as individuals, and for groups of people—the members of the team—to strive to achieve the team's performance objectives. This creates an environment where everybody can be a winner, both individually and as team members.

Good teams, organizations, and companies become great ones when the members trust each other enough to focus their energies on We instead of Me.

REMEMBER

The power of We is stronger than the power of Me.

Think of everybody with whom you come in contact as a teammate or a potential teammate. Teamwork is the essence of life. When one team member does something well and succeeds, everybody wins. Be a team player. When your team wins, you win. And don't think only of winning games, but of winning championships!

Asking For and Getting Help When You Need It

It's much easier to be successful in any endeavor when you have the help and assistance of others. You'll get much better results when you *ask* a person to do something instead of *demanding, dictating,* or *telling* him what to do.

Encourage and motivate people in such a way that you're able to get them to want to do what you want them to do. With the help of others, you'll be able to spend your time and energies on other work, tasks, and projects.

One of the big advantages of having teammates comes from the fact that you don't have to do *all* the work yourself. For most of us it's impossible to get the job done without the assistance of others.

So when you ask someone for help, use a very soft, subtle, low-key approach. These are some phrases you can use when you ask someone to do something for you:

- "I'm sorry to trouble you, but . . ."
- "Would you be so kind as to . . ."
- "Would you please . . ."
- "Would you mind doing . . ."
- "If I may ask a favor of you, would you please . . ."
- "I know you're very busy, but . . ."

The Art of Delegating

Once you've asked someone to do something, you just can't walk away from the task. You need to make sure it's done properly and completed on time. Here are some tips you can use to guarantee that delegated tasks are done properly and completed on time.

- **Explain What Needs to Be Done.** When you delegate a task, take the time to explain to the person exactly what you want him to do. Make sure the person *understands* what needs to be done.

REMEMBER

The person certainly wants to do a good job, but you have the responsibility to make sure the proper information has been conveyed to him as to what your expectations are.

- **Give a Due Date.** Give the person a specific date and/or time by which the work needs to be completed. For example, you could tell the person the report needs to be on your desk by 4:00 P.M. on Tuesday or 9:00 A.M. on Thursday.

- **Ask the Person to Assume Responsibility.** Once you've explained what needs to be done and when it needs to be completed, ask for the person's commitment to completing the task. You can say something like: "This is very important to me; can I count on you to complete it by . . . ?" By doing this you are asking the person to assume responsibility for the successful completion of this task or project within the given time frame.

● **Provide the Necessary Resources.** When you assign a task, it's your responsibility to make sure the person is provided with the proper resources. This could include equipment and materials, the assistance of colleagues and/or co-workers, and other financial resources if necessary.

● **Explain the Criteria for Evaluation.** Discuss with the person the standards of performance that will be used to evaluate whether or not the job was done properly. In addition, explain what will happen as a result of the evaluation.

● **You *Must* Follow Up.** Once the person starts work on the task, you should follow up on a regular basis to make sure things are moving in the right direction and at the proper pace. This can be done easily by adding the item to your Master List or scheduling a follow-up inside ACT!. But remember to give the delegatee the opportunity to make his or her own decisions as to how to go about getting the job done. The only thing that matters is the quality of work that's produced and the timeliness in which it goes out the door. Trust that others are capable of getting the job done.

● **Show Appreciation for a Job Well Done.** When the project or task has been successfully completed, remember to say "Thank You," and compliment the person for a job well done. Make people feel important and let them know how much you appreciate their contributions.

 REMEMBER

People want to do their jobs and do them well. And they want to be associated with a successful organization.

Share the Limelight

Share the limelight, prestige, recognition, credit, power, and profits with those who helped in the successful completion of the work, task, or project. Make your other contributors feel important. Do everything you can to make those around you look good. Bask in the reflected glory of the successes and accomplishments of your friends, colleagues, and co-workers. Share in their successes, and let them share in yours. There's plenty for everybody.

REMEMBER

Praise the person in public, and criticize the process in private.

Become a Brilliant Conversationalist

Successful people are successful because they know how to get what they want. And the way you go about asking people for the things you want can have a dramatic effect on your ability to get those things. You start by becoming a brilliant conversationalist, and the easiest way to do this is by becoming a better listener.

But what is listening? Listening is an art. Listening is an activity. Listening is being *sincerely* interested in hearing what the other person has to say. For it is by listening that you learn what another person is thinking and feeling.

How do you become a better listener? By encouraging the other person to talk. Yes, people love to talk about themselves, so let them. Ask a person a question, listen to the answer, and then ask another question. In no time at all you'll learn all about people's personal and family lives, their business affairs, business activities and ongoing business relationships, your competition, and almost anything else you can imagine.

When you listen to people, you're letting them know you value them and their thoughts and ideas. When you listen attentively, you are paying the highest of compliments. You are showing people that you are genuinely interested in hearing what they have to say. For you get to know others by talking about the things that they want to talk about.

Here are two additional things to remember:

- It takes only 15 percent of the brain to process and understand language, so you have 85 percent of your attention available to really listen.

● You'll go further in life by being a good listener than being a good talker. When was the last time you heard someone say: "I *listened* myself out of a sale"?

The Art of Asking Questions

When you ask a question, listen to the answer and then ask a follow-up question. This is how you learn what the other person is thinking and feeling. Questions help you to identify the person's real wants and needs. Questions help you to identify a person's goals, dreams, and desires. Questions help you to identify existing problems that you can help solve. Questions help you to discover potential opportunities.

So when you ask a person a question, ask a question he or she will enjoy answering.

Always Ask Open-Ended Questions

Brilliant conversationalists always ask open-ended questions. And what is an open-ended question? It's a question that encourages the other person to talk and share his or her innermost thoughts and feelings. To ask an open-ended question, all you've got to do is phrase your question in such a way that it includes a

● **Who**

● **What**

● **When**

● **Why**

● **Where**

● **How**

When you ask open-ended questions you're showing that you are sincerely interested in what people have to say. You are not only encouraging people to continue speaking, thus keeping the conversation going, but you're giving them the opportunity to fully explain their thoughts, opinions, comments, and feelings. With an open-ended question, you're asking people to give you an informative and descriptive answer. Ask your question in the right way and you'll be amazed at how much information people are willing to volunteer.

Now I must admit it's not always easy to phrase a question with a Who, What, When, Why, Where, or How. But that's what makes it fun and challenging. When you're working at phrasing questions that encourage people to continue speaking, you become an active participant in the conversation. It shows people you're truly interested in hearing what they have to say, and they open up even further. Once they realize you are willing to take the time to understand them, true communication begins to take place.

SUCCESS TIP

Each time you speak with a person, try to ask three questions of him before you start speaking about yourself. This will show that you are interested in the person and the things that are going on in his life.

REMEMBER

When you talk about yourself, you're a bore. Talk to other people about themselves, and they'll listen for hours. Encourage others to talk about the things they most treasure, and you've become a brilliant conversationalist.

Here are two additional thoughts about how to ask questions:

- **Avoid Asking Closed-Ended Questions.** When a question is asked that can be answered with a simple Yes or No, the conversation dies. You just can't have a meaningful conversation when all you're getting is yes or no answers. Your challenge is to figure out new and creative ways in which you can phrase your questions so that they include the words Who, What, When, Why, Where, or How.

- **Always Ask Questions in a Positive Way.** When you ask a question, always phrase it in a positive way. This helps to ensure that the course, mood, tone, and flow of a conversation continue in the right direction. You always want to talk about things from a positive perspective. For example, you could say, "What would you like to see improved?" instead of saying, "What don't you like about . . ." Or you could say, "What should I have done differently?" or "How could I have done it better?" rather than saying, "What did I do wrong?"

Listen to Understand What the Other Person Is Saying

As you're engaging the person in conversation, listen with your whole body. Sit up straight, lean forward slightly, and as the other person is speaking look at the person's face and watch his body language. Listen with your eyes, your mind, your heart, your whole body, in addition to your ears. Listen for the words between the words. Listen for feeling. Listen for meaning.

Try to understand and absorb the things the other person is saying. Give the other person your undivided attention as you weigh each word, each sentence, and each phrase.

Spoken words—along with hand, face, eye, and body movements— make up a dialogue. When the words a person speaks and the movements of his or her body are in rhythm, they strengthen and underscore meaning.

Pay particular attention to the silence between the words. When people pause, let the silence linger; don't interrupt their train of thought or finish the sentence for them. Give them the opportunity to speak with their own words.

As you listen, look for the subtle messages the other person sends, then try to interpret and understand what those messages really mean.

Watch the person's facial expressions. Is he smiling or frowning? Are the muscles in his face, forehead, and jaw relaxed or tense? And watch his eyes. What is he looking at? What are his eyes focusing on? (When you look someone in the eye, focus on only one eye. When you try to focus on both eyes, your own eyes move from right to left.)

What is the person doing with her body? Is she leaning forward or reclining backward? Is she calm and relaxed, stiff as a board, or fidgeting like a worm at the end of the hook?

What is the position of the person's arms? Are they open or folded across his chest? What is he doing with his hands and his fingers? What about his legs? Are they relaxed, or does he change positions every few moments? And what are his feet doing?

REMEMBER

The spoken word represents only 10 percent of your ability to communicate. Another 30 percent is represented by the tone of your voice as you speak those words. The remaining 60 percent of your communication skills is represented by the movement of your body.

Here are some additional tips that will help you to become a better listener:

- **Nod Your Head.** Nod as you listen to a person speak. This indicates that you heard and understood what the person said—though it does not necessarily mean that you are in agreement—and encourages him to continue speaking. You can also say such things as: "*Oh*," "*Uh-huh*," "*That's interesting*," "*I see*," or "*Mmmm*."

- **Use the Person's Name.** When asking a question or responding to a statement, use the other person's name as you encourage him to continue speaking. You could say something like: "*Sharon, would you tell me more . . .*" or "*Jim, what happened next?*" or "*Then what did you do, Mitzi?*"

- **Repeat the Statement.** For further clarification, repeat the things you have just heard. This lets the speaker know you have been trying to understand him. You can say something like: "*If I heard you correctly, you said . . .*" or "*I just want to make sure I understand what you just said . . .*"

- **Ask Follow-up Questions.** When a person says something, ask a follow-up question. Be curious about people's ideas and thought processes. Be interested in what they have to say. Don't jump from one subject to another. When you change subjects immediately after a person makes a statement, you're indicating that you really aren't interested in what he has to say. There is no communication. There is no flow of ideas. There is no feedback.

ANECDOTE

This is one of my biggest pet peeves: I'm talking with someone and he or she asks: *"How are you doing?"* or *"What's going on?"* So I answer, and instead of asking a follow-up question, the person says, *"Well, what else is going on?"* The conversation goes on this way for about 45 seconds and it's apparent that this person has absolutely no interest in any of the things that are going on in my life.

● **Pay Attention.** Concentrate, pay attention, and listen to the things the other person is saying. Work to keep your mind from wandering. Let people fully express themselves. Let them finish their thoughts. Try to control your desire to speak.

REMEMBER

● Don't interrupt or cut the person off. When you interrupt people, you're responding to them or contradicting them before they've even completed their statement.

● When someone is presenting a new idea, wait until you've heard the whole idea and have had time to think about its merits before you pass judgment as to whether it's good or bad. It's far too easy to criticize an idea and find reasons why something shouldn't be done.

● **Be Courteous and Show Respect.** Listen respectfully to everything that is being said, even if you don't agree. After the person has finished speaking, you can then ask additional questions or respond to the previous statement.

REMEMBER

If you have no respect for the speaker, don't waste your time and energy engaging in a conversation. You'll only end up angry and frustrated. Do your best to end the conversation as quickly as possible.

- **Don't Be Judgmental.** Let the person make his case. Be impartial as you weigh what he or she is saying against what you know. Though it's only natural to try to anticipate where the speaker is going, don't be so concerned with responding to his last statement that you're no longer listening to what is being said. And don't impose your own agenda on the other person. Set aside your own prejudices, frames of reference, and desires so you can experience—as far as possible—what is happening inside the other person's world.

- **Control Yourself.** When a person is saying things that you don't agree with, try your best to control yourself. Don't get excited. Don't get upset. Don't get angry.

- **Stop Whatever You're Doing.** When someone wants to talk to you, stop doing whatever you're doing and listen to what the person has to say. Put everything aside for a few moments—including your own thoughts, worries, and preoccupations—and *listen* to the other person.

- **Keep People's Trust.** When someone speaks to you in confidence, you have an obligation to maintain his trust. In any relationship or organization, trust is the emotional glue that binds people together. Trust is a basic ingredient of any successful organization, and it must be earned. And once trust is earned, you must work twice as hard to keep it.

- **Don't Probe.** Probing is asking questions without really being interested in the answers. Probing follows a logical line of questioning that doesn't encourage the other person to be open. It doesn't encourage communication.

- **Don't Take Telephone Calls.** When you're having a conversation, don't interrupt the conversation by taking a telephone call. It's insulting to the other person, destroys the conversation's flow, and wastes the other person's time.

- **Don't Doodle.** Doodling, either during a meeting or when you're on the phone, indicates you're no longer listening or paying attention to the other person.

The Art of Negotiating

Every day you and I are negotiating with other people. Some of these negotiations are big and important, but the majority are just day-to-day living. For example, when my daughter comes home from school, she wants a can of soda. I say no and offer her some apple juice. She says she wants grape juice. I pour it for her.

When my wife comes in, we have our usual discussion about what to eat for dinner. She wants Japanese, I want a hamburger, and my daughter wants Chinese. We settle on Mexican.

When I negotiated the contract for this book with my editor, I had a long list of things I wanted included in the contract, and she had a long list of things she wanted included in the contract. As we went over each item on our respective lists, we discovered that some items were more important than others. And we also discovered that a number of items were important to one of us, but not to both of us. Little by little we worked our way through our lists and eventually came to an agreement.

No, I didn't get *all* of the things I wanted, but I did get a contract to write a book with a fine publisher. And I know my editor wasn't happy giving me *all* of the provisions that I did manage to get, but she got what she wanted, the opportunity to publish a book with a good, hard-working author. In the end we both felt like winners because we both got what we wanted: a contract to write this book.

SUCCESS TIP

Kare Anderson's *Getting What You Want* (Plume/Penguin) is one of the best books I've ever read on how to negotiate. Her newest book is *Resolve Conflicts Sooner* (The Crossing Press). Kare is one of America's leading experts on persuasion and negotiating techniques. For more information, you can reach her at 415-331-6336 or visit her Web site at www.sayitbetter.com.

Know What You Want

Before you get into a negotiation with a person, you must know what it is you want. For example, if you are going into a meeting with your boss and you want a raise, think about all the other things you may also want. Put a lot of items on the table and then play Let's Make a Deal.

In addition to an increase in salary, you could ask for more flexible work hours, extra vacation time, extended holiday time, additional life insurance, a membership at a health club, or the opportunity to travel to some business meetings or conventions.

With many items from which to choose, the likelihood that you can create a package you both can live with is greatly increased.

If you're in sales, when a customer asks for a lower price, don't just cut your price without getting something in return. Perhaps you can get the customer to increase the size of his order. Maybe you can change the payment terms and get a larger deposit or even a prepayment. Or maybe you can change the scheduled delivery dates.

When you're able to introduce a number of variables into a negotiation—some very important, others of lesser importance—the probability that you'll be able to close a deal is greatly increased.

Look at the Situation from the Other Person's Point of View

Once you begin negotiating, get into the other person's shoes. Put yourself in his place. Look at the situation from the other person's point of view. When you know the answers to these questions:

- What does he want?

- What does he need?

- What is important to him?

- What are his goals?

- What are his objectives and priorities?

You'll be in a much better position to find a mutually agreeable solution or resolution to the situation or problem.

Once these issues have been laid out on the table, they can then be discussed, negotiated, and resolved one by one.

 **SUCCESS TIP**

Search for the other person's hidden agendas. Try to discover the things that are *really* important to him.

Here are some tips that will help you in any negotiation:

- **Identify the Key Issues and Areas of Concern.** On a pad of paper, make a list of each item that is important to you and each item that is important to the other person.

- **Look for Points of Agreement.** Study your lists and look for areas of agreement or similarities in your positions. Once you find areas of agreement, you can build upon them.

  Your goal is to get the other person to start saying YES. The more YESses you get, the greater the likelihood that you'll come to an agreement. Get other people to say YES enough times, and they'll start to embrace your position as they begin to give up their own.

  Listen to what the other person is saying, and ask additional questions. Let the other person talk himself out of objections. As he talks, you listen. Ask more questions. Listen. Ask more questions.

- **Identify the Specific Points on Which You Don't Agree.** Write down each of these points on a pad of paper. Record where each of you stands on every point. How far apart are you on each of these items? Try to understand why the two of you differ.

- **Look for More Options.** Look for new options or solutions that can help the person achieve the results he is looking for. If you ask enough questions, you will find that there are things that are important to the other person that aren't very important to you. And there will be things that are important to you that aren't very important to the other person. So trade an unimportant item for an important item. Your objective is to create the opportunity for each of you to get what you want so you both walk away winners.

- **Plant Seeds.** The best way to get the things you want is to make the other person think, feel, or believe the idea was his idea. That the solution to this problem was his solution.

  You can do this by casually and subtly planting seeds in the person's mind so you can get him thinking about the situation. Talk about the things he wants, and then show him how to get them. This is a very effective way to influence people.

REMEMBER

Getting results is more important than getting credit.

- **Develop Trust.** Trust makes communication possible. Trust implies accountability, predictability, and reliability. Be honest about how you feel on every issue under negotiation.

- **Lighten Up.** Humor is a very powerful negotiating tool. It's disarming, it lightens a highly charged atmosphere, and it can be very helpful in cutting or reducing tension. Often the use of humor can strengthen your hand.

- **Think Things Over.** Give yourself time to think. In most situations it isn't necessary to make an immediate decision. When you give yourself time to think things through, you can weigh the pros and cons of the issues being discussed. In addition, you'll be able to judge the impact one item may have upon another.

REMEMBER

When you tell a person you want time to think things over, discuss how much time you need and set a specific date by which you'll get back to the person.

You may also want to schedule another meeting to discuss these items further. This gives each of you an opportunity to think about the other's positions and areas of concern.

- **Thank the Person for His Interest.** If he weren't interested, the person wouldn't be involved in a conversation, discussion, or negotiation. He would have just walked away.

- **Know When to Say, "No Deal."** When you know what you want, you're in a position to determine what results would constitute a fully acceptable resolution to the discussion or negotiation. If in the end you're unable to resolve the issues so that you—and presumably the other person—feel good about the decisions that have been made, then it's best to walk away and say, "No deal."

Make Everybody Feel Like a Winner

As you go through life, try to make everybody with whom you come in contact feel like a winner. Follow this approach and you'll find that all of your business and personal relationships are mutually beneficial and satisfying. You'll eliminate confrontation and work together with your colleagues, co-workers, customers, clients, suppliers, and everybody else in a collaborative manner as you try to achieve a common goal.

Approach each conversation, interaction, or negotiation with another person as an opportunity to cooperate with him. Your attitude should be:

"I want you to get what's most important to you,
AND I want to get what's most important to me."

You will have found a way for both of you to get the things you want and feel good about it.

With this attitude you become collaborators instead of competitors. You're working together as friends who want to achieve a common goal. And when the discussions are over, everybody should feel good about the mutual decisions that have been made.

REMEMBER

The best business deal isn't the one that maximizes your advantage or your profits. It's the one in which you maximize the chance that the next time you run into the person you'll be glad to see each other.

Don't Get into an Argument

When you're having a conversation with someone, the last thing you want to do is get into an argument. Anger clouds your mind and impairs your ability to think clearly. Once you start arguing, your position hardens, the other person's position hardens, and it becomes impossible to find a mutually agreeable solution or resolution to the issues being discussed.

When the other person is angry, don't take the bait and get into an argument. Listen patiently. Though you'll certainly be tempted to interrupt and respond to the person's statements, stay calm and say nothing. Within a few minutes the person will use up all of his anger, dissipate his energy, and talk himself out. Now that he has calmed down, you can have an intelligent conversation.

Your goal and objective is to find a reasonable solution to the problem. When you're angry, you won't achieve the desired result if you get into a shouting match, pick up the phone—or go down the hall—and tell the other person what a !@#$*% he is. So when you're angry, give yourself time to cool off.

Here are some additional thoughts on the benefits of avoiding an argument:

- A misunderstanding is never ended satisfactorily by an argument. It is done by tact, diplomacy, conciliation, and a sympathetic desire to see things from the other person's point of view. This will help you achieve much better results, as well as the goodwill of the other person.

- If you come at people with your fists clenched, ready for a fight, they'll prepare themselves for battle. You can't force someone to agree with you, but you can gently lead him along the path toward agreement. Gentleness and friendliness are always stronger than force and fury.

- The best way to win an argument is to avoid it.

- When you're angry and you want to write a letter, write it, but don't mail it. Put it in a drawer for a day or two. Talk about the situation with a close friend or family member. When you look at the letter a day later, you'll probably decide you don't want to put it in the mail.

- Never make a business decision based upon an emotional reaction. Always give yourself time to cool off before you make a decision.

But I'm Right . . .

Many times during a conversation you'll know that you're right and the other person is wrong. But don't spend so much time, energy, and emotion building up your position that you haven't left the other person an opening to graciously admit that he is wrong, so that he can come around to your position.

Your goal is to try to win the other person to your way of thinking. But do it gently and tactfully. Always let the other person save face. Never embarrass him. If the other person doesn't have a way to admit that he is wrong and save face, he will continue defending his position until hell freezes over.

And it doesn't do you any good to tell the person that he is wrong and rub his nose in it. In fact, a lot of damage can be done, because it may make the person more stirred up, upset, and angry. And though you may be dead right in your argument, when it's all over, you no longer have a friend, and you no longer have a relationship.

My dad used to recite to me this poem:

Remember the story of Johnny Day,
Who died defending his right of way.
He was right, dead right, as he sped along,
But he's just as dead as if he were wrong.

When You're Wrong

When you're wrong, admit your mistakes. Apologize to the people who were affected and let them know that you are sincerely sorry about what happened. (Hopefully, the other people will leave you an opening to graciously admit that you were wrong.) Explain the steps you will take to correct the mistake and/or resolve the problem so that the other people will be satisfied with the results. And outline the steps you will take to ensure that the same thing won't happen again. If this is satisfactory to the other people, don't dwell on this problem any longer and make it a point to move on.

Make the Most out of Every Day

Strive to do your very best. And as you work harder, and your skills and talents improve, you'll find that you get better and better at the things you do. Tasks that were difficult yesterday are easier today. Tomorrow they won't even be challenging. This is called personal growth and improvement. And no matter where you are on your personal learning curve, there is always room for growth and improvement.

However, as you grow, develop, and expand your skills and talents, you'll find that you move forward one small step at a time. In life, there really aren't that many opportunities for huge changes, and you shouldn't expect them for yourself. For must of us, improvement comes in small increments. Just concentrate on moderate, sustainable growth and improvement.

Do Things ¼ of a Percent Better Each Day

Work to improve your daily processes and procedures. Think about everything you do during the course of your workday. As you're doing each task, ask yourself this question: "How can I do this just a little bit faster and better?"

You don't have to try to make huge geometric gains; a lot of tiny ones will be sufficient. Improve your daily performance by just ¼ of a percent each day and you'll have a huge increase in your results. You'll be 1 percent better at the end of each week, 12 percent better at the end of the quarter, and 50 percent better at the end of the year. Do that over and over and you've had yourself a great life and career.

Set Daily Goals for Yourself

When people set goals for themselves, they're usually looking at long-term goals. I think of long-term goals as a kind of wish list. People want to do *this*, and they want to do *that*, and they want to accomplish their goals by a specific date.

However, the thing most people fail to do is devise a plan of action that enables them to do the things necessary to make their dreams come true. Without a well-executed plan, the goals are nothing but a pipe dream.

In order to achieve your goals and make your dreams and wishes come true, you've got to break those goals into the smallest common denominator. You need to maintain a much narrower focus. Once you finish a task, you need to look at your Master List and ask yourself: "What is the most important task that I need to do?" Do it now!

REMEMBER

A journey of a thousand miles begins with a single step . . . forward.

The thing you must always keep in mind is how you are using your time at this very moment. Are the work, tasks, and projects you're in the process of completing going to take you where you want to go? It is for this reason that I feel proper planning is so very important.

SUCCESS TIP

It's much easier to accomplish the things you want when you have a well-thought-out and well-executed plan of action.

Set daily goals for yourself, and break them down even further. Before you go home tonight, ask yourself: "What do I want to accomplish tomorrow?" But don't leave it at that. That's too broad. What do you want to accomplish tomorrow morning? What tasks do you want to complete by 9:00 A.M.? 10:00 A.M.? 11:00 A.M.?

Be specific. Set immediate deadlines. Don't allow yourself to be interrupted. Stay focused.

Have a Great Day, Every Day

Plan to have a great, productive, and rewarding day every day. Start planning next week on Thursday or Friday of this week. Review your Master List in detail. Identify the work, tasks, and projects that are most important—the ones that will have the biggest payoff. Write those tasks on your calendar and block out the time, and plan to work on them first thing Monday morning.

When you arrive on Monday morning, sit down at your desk, pull out the appropriate files, turn off the telephone, close the door (if you don't have a door, put out a Do Not Disturb sign), and go to work. Knock off one important task one after another after another. Set yourself up to have a highly productive—and GREAT—Monday morning *and* afternoon. Before you leave in the afternoon, review your Master List and identify the most important tasks you need to tackle so you can have a GREAT Tuesday.

Follow this process each day, and before you know it you've had a GREAT week, a GREAT month, a GREAT quarter, and a GREAT year. Continue this process year after year after year and you will have a GREAT career.

> **REMEMBER**
>
> It all starts with the idea of having a great Monday morning.

Strive for Excellence

Strive for excellence in everything you do. Excellence is about consistently high performance. Excellence is about knowing how much to give and the right time to give it. Excellence is the gradual result of always wanting to do better. As a leader you must always encourage those around you to strive to do their best.

So as you strive for excellence, just set your sights on the next rung on the ladder. When you reach it, set your sights one rung higher. And when you reach that rung, set your sights one rung higher. Before you know it you've gone farther, and done more things, than you ever thought possible.

Think Winning Thoughts

As you go through life, fill your mind with positive thoughts, winning thoughts. Think of all the things you can do, that you're capable of doing, that you're dreaming of doing. Think of your mind as a fertile garden. Fill your mind with positive, uplifting, encouraging thoughts, and you will have an abundant crop of success.

Fill your mind with words and thoughts that energize you and motivate you to succeed. Use words like:

I can . . .
I will . . .
I am going to . . .

As my good friend Bill Fletcher used to say: *"Success comes in cans. Not cannots."*

Surround Yourself with Positive, Supportive People

Surround yourself with positive, supportive, and encouraging people. People who bring you up. People who believe in you. People who cherish your friendship. People who bask in the reflected glory of your success. People who share in your dreams and want to help you make your dreams come true.

In closing, I would like to leave you with one of my favorite poems.

If you think you are beaten, you are,
If you think you dare not, you don't.
If you like to win, but you think you can't,
It is almost certain you won't.

If you think you'll lose, you've lost,
For out in the world you'll find,
Success begins with a fellow's will—
It's all in the state of mind.

If you think you are outclassed, you are,
You've got to think high to rise,
You've got to be sure of yourself before
You can ever win *the* Prize.

Life's battles don't always go
To the stronger or faster man,
But soon or later the man who wins
Is the man **Who *Knows* He Can!**

—ANONYMOUS

INDEX

Academy awards, 32
Accomplishments, 41–42
ACT!:
    attachments with, 145
    Contact window in, 79, 142
    conversations inside, 55
    e-mail and, 145
    following up with, 86
    History file in, 146, 147
    Internet surfing with, 146
    notepads with, 143, 156
    palmtop computers and, 88–89
    personal information with, 78–80,
        140–147, 164
    Phone List dialog box in, 146
    printing information from, 89
    Schedule Activity box for, 81
    scheduling activities with, 81–88,
        147
    setting alarms with, 88
    Task List, 84, 147
    tracking customers with, 161
    unfinished activities, 87, 147
    value of, 77–78
    viewing tasks as list, 84–85
    viewing tasks by person, 82–83
    viewing tasks on calendar, 85
    WinFax PRO and, 145
    writing letters with, 144, 147–148

Action, converting talk into, 27–28
Address books, disadvantages to,
    137
Addresses, keeping track of, 80
Adversity, 37–38
Agenda(s):
    example of, 118
    hidden, 180
    importance of, 116–117
Airplanes, 131, 132
Ali, Muhammad, 31
Ambition, as requirement for suc-
    cessful people, 15
Anderson, Kare, 179
Apologies, 185
Appointments with oneself, 111–112
Appreciation, importance of show-
    ing, 171
Arguments, avoiding, 183–185
Army Medical Corps, 38
Asking questions, art of, 173–175
Assistance, gaining, 169–170
Attention, importance of paying,
    177

Baseball, 26–27, 31, 92
Basketball, 9–10
Belluzzo, Richard E., 8
Berra, Yogi, 50

Bills:
  paying, 2
  paying company, 7
Blankers-Koen, Fanny, 23
Bojaxhiu, Agnes, 43
Boss, getting to know your,
  157–158
Business cards, 78–79
  disadvantages to files of, 137–138
  exchanging, 132
  importance of obtaining, 155
  scanning, 138

Calcutta, India, 43
Calendar, blocking out time on,
  112
  during meetings, 117
  for you, 115
  (*See also* ACT!; Schedule)
Caray, Harry, 26–27
Career, finding a good, 25
Case History sheets, 139
Chemistry between people, 132,
  156–157
Chicago Bulls, 9
Chicago Cubs, 26
Chicago White Sox, 26
Churchill, Winston, 23
Cleaning, 61–63
Clinton, Bill, 130
Cohn, Ted, 163
Colleagues, scheduling time with,
  121
Color-coding files, 68
Commitment, 22
Commuting to work, 97
Company success, 7
Complimenting, importance of,
  171–172
Computer:
  laptop, 1

Computer (*Cont.*):
  Master List into, 77–80
  name and address book into,
    139–144
Conference calls, 120–121
Conferences, business, 132
Connections (*see* Networking)
Considine, Ray, 163
Contact Data Entry, 138
Contact managers, 78
Contracts, negotiating, 179
Conversationalist, becoming a bril-
  liant, 172–174
Cook, Edmund Vance, 39
Coolidge, Calvin, 30
Cooperation, 17
Crises, managing, 105
Customers:
  being available for, 113
  most profitable, 160–162

Daily Agenda Sheet, 124–126
Daily Efficiency Chart, 114
Darjeeling, India, 43
DAZ-zle, 145
DDB Needham, 21
Deadlines, setting, 102–103, 188
Decisions, making, 16
Defeat, reacting to, 37–38
Delegating, art of, 170–171
Denver Broncos, 29
Desire(s), 2
  prioritizing according to, 99
  of successful people, 27–29
Desk:
  cleaning, 61–63
  lap drawer of, 138
  organizing drawers of, 64–65
Desk file drawer, 65–66
  (*See also* Master file drawer)
Details, importance of, 51

Disagreement, 178
  identifying points of, 181
  (*See also* Arguments, avoiding)
Documents, writing and proofread-
  ing, 104
Doodling, 178
Doubt, 36
Dream(s), 2
  list of, 99
  prioritizing according to, 99
  of successful people, 14–15,
    21–24
Due date, importance of giving, 170

Edison, Thomas, 34
Effectiveness, 106
Efficiency, 106
Ellison, Lawrence J., 8
Elway, John, 29
E-mail:
  with ACT!, 145
  checking, 1
Enthusiasm, 17
Envelope Manager Software, 145
Evaluation, explaining criteria for,
  171
Excellence, striving for, 189–190
Expandable file pockets, 68–69
Expectations:
  exceeding, 103
  success depends on, 4–5
Eyes, looking into, 175

Facial expression, 133
Failure(s):
  importance of not accepting, 30
  learning from, 34, 35
  not being afraid of, 33–36
  overcoming fear of, 35
Faith, 29–30
False security in sales, 160–161

Family, 2
Favre, Brett, 29
Faxes, 1
  with ACT!, 145
Fear, six symptoms of, 36
File(s):
  disadvantages to Rolodex,
    134–136
  organizing, 65–67
  reading, 69–70
  resources, 69, 71
File folders, 67–69
Fires, putting out, 1, 105
First impressions, 133
Focus, 15
Following up:
  importance of, 171
  system for, 86
  (*See also* ACT!, following up
    with)
Football, 11, 29
Friends:
  art of making, 131, 150–153, 156,
    166
  of Bill Clinton, 130
  friends of, 154–155
  information about, 165–166
  most important, 151
  selecting, 133–134, 156–157
Friendship, 130
  (*See also* Friends; Networking)
Fulfillment, 2

Getting What You Want, 179
Glenn, John, 21
Goals, 2, 3
  importance of daily, 187–188
  list of, 99
  prioritizing according to, 99
  writing down, 4, 50
Godfather, The, 31–32

Goldin, Daniel S., 21
Goldmine, 78
Golf, 10
Grades, 5
Great Britain, 23
Green Bay Packers, 29
Growth, personal, 187

Habits, pleasing, 16
Hanging folders, 68
Happiness, 16
Hewlett-Packard, 8
Homecourt, 9
Hornberger, H. Richard, 38
Hotels, storing information about,
   143
How Did You Die, 39
How to Work a Room, 133
Humor, 182

Improvement, personal, 187–190
In-box, 1
   organizing, 64
Indecision, 36
Indifference, 36
Internet, searching, 1, 146
Interruptions, avoid causing, 177
It's A Wonderful Life, 7

Jackson, Phil, 9
Job(s):
   finding a good, 25
   keeping track of people who
      change, 136
Jordan, Michael, 9
Journal, keeping, 127–128
Junk drawer, 64

Keating, Linda, 82
Korean War, 38
Kroc, Ray, 21, 23

Label printers, 69
Letters, 1
   with ACT!, 144
   importance of keeping short,
      104
Life insurance, 6
Lightbulb, invention of, 34
Lincoln, Abraham, 104
Listening:
   importance of, 172
   techniques, 175–178
Luck, of successful people, 30–33

Mail, 1
   merges with ACT!, 145
M*A*S*H, 38
Master file drawer, 66–67
Master List:
   adding new items to, 73
   inside computer, 77–80
   consolidating the pages of, 74, 87
   and Daily Agenda Sheet, 124
   doing one more task on, 97
   importance of, 72
   listing tasks on, 63, 72
   most important tasks on, 188
   noting reading material on, 70
   recording everything on, 75
   shortcomings of, 81
   (*See also* ACT!)
Master Plan of ACTion, 2
   Board of Directors, 53
   constantly changing, 52–53
   criticizing, 54–55
   importance of, 48
   speaking with people about,
      53–56
   as time saver, 49–50
   writing, 50–52
Maximizer, 78
McDonald's, 21, 23

Meeting people, increasing opportunities for, 131–132
Meetings, 1, 95, 116–117
  avoiding impromptu, 119–120
  with your colleagues, 121–122
Microsoft Word, 51
Mistakes, 16–17
  admitting, 185
  cost money, 103, 104
Morning, working in the, 114
Mother Teresa, 43
Motivation, 15
MVP, 9

Name(s), 164
  remembering, 154–155
  using, 176
NASA, 21
Naysayers, get rid of, 24, 56
Negotiating:
  art of, 179–182
  looking for agreement, 181
  when to walk away from, 182
Netherlands, 23
Networking, 54–55
  with ACT!, 140–148
  art of, 150–153
  with your boss, 157–158
  definition of, 131
  within your industry, 159
  lifelong process of, 156–157
  within your organization,
    157–159
  with paper-based systems,
    134–138
New York Jets, 11
Numbers, checking, 105

Obsession, turning your dream into,
  28
Olympics, 9, 23

Oracle corporation, 8
Out-box, 1
  organizing, 64
Overcautiousness, 36
Owens, Jesse, 23

Papers:
  dating, 74
  going through, 63–64
Parcells, Bill, 11
Parents, 5
Passion, 22
People:
  attractive qualities of, 153
  building relationships with, 30
  business information of, 165
  friends of most important,
    154–155
  to get to know better, 152
  increasing opportunities for
    meeting, 131–132
  within your industry, 159
  most important, 151
  within your organization,
    157–159
  personal information of, 165–166
  (See also Networking; Supportive
    people)
Perseverance, 30
Persistence, 33–34
Personal information storage, 78–80
  (See also ACT!; Addresses, keeping
    track of; Business cards; Case
    History sheets; Rolodex file)
Personnel transitions, coping with,
  163
Phone (see Telephone)
Pippen, Scottie, 9
Planning:
  importance of, 48
  for tomorrow, 74

Planning (*Cont.*):
  (*See also* ACT!; Master Plan of
    ACTion)
Plexus Corporation, 8
Politics, 166
Positive thinking, 189–190
Practice, 36
Prime time, 113–115
Priorities:
  importance of, 61
  scheduling, 106
  setting, 99–101
Private time, scheduling, 111–112,
    114
Problem solving, 5–6, 16, 107
  accepting responsibility for, 109
  importance of taking time for,
    108
Procrastination, 36
  as career-killer, 101
  exacerbates problems, 108
  successful people stay away from,
    100
Productivity, 15
  daily, 188–189
  different than busyness, 49
Proofreading, importance of, 104
Proposals, 1
Publicity, 141–142

Questions:
  avoiding closed-ended, 174
  follow-up, 176
  importance of asking, 173
  open-ended, 173–174
  positive, 174–175
Quitting, 36–38

Reading file, 69–70
Recognition, 171–172
Redemption, 32

Reinhard, Keith, 21
Relationships, 130
  with all people in organization,
    163
Reminders, 62, 65
Resolve Conflicts Sooner, 179
Resources:
  file, 69, 71
  providing necessary, 171
Respect, importance of showing, 177
Responsibility, 16, 103
  asking a person to assume,
    170–171
Restaurants, storing information
    about, 142
Results, pleasing, 16
Rocky, 31–32
Rolodex file:
  disadvantages of, 134–136
  replacing, 83
  transferring business card infor-
    mation to, 132
Runner-up, 8

Sales, 6, 160–162
  luck in, 32
  negotiation in, 180
Sanders, Barry, 11
Satisfaction, 2
Scanner, business card, 138
Schedule:
  activities in, 152
  appointments with yourself,
    111–112
  for the day, 123–124
  proper priorities of, 106
  telephone calls in, 120–121
  time with colleagues in, 121–122
  (*See also* ACT!)
School functions, 132
Schrage, Paul, 21

Seiko Instruments, 69, 138
Self-discipline, 15
Self-reliance, 17
Seminars, business, 132
Senior citizens, 21
Shaking hands, 133
Sharkware, 78
Shire, Talia, 32
Silicon Graphics, 8
Sinatra, Frank, 33
Sisters of Loretto, 43
Skills and talents, 43–45
Smart Business Card Reader, 138
Smiling, importance of, 133, 155
Space travel, 21
Staff, scheduling time with, 121–122
  (*See also* People, within your
    organization)
Stallone, Sylvester, 31–32
Stewart, James, 7
Sticky notes, 1, 64
St. Louis Cardinals, 26
Stock market, 8
Stocks, 7
Success, 2
  company, 7
  criteria for, 10
  definition of, 4–6
  dependent on expectations, 4
  eight principles of, 20
  nonlinear, 3
  paying price for, 58
  as result of participation, 11
  in sales, 6
  state of mind for, 14
Successful people:
  admit mistakes, 16
  aren't afraid of failure, 33–36
  are persistent, 38
  characteristics of, 14–17
  don't procrastinate, 100

Successful people (*Cont.*):
  don't quit, 36–38
  have ambition, 15
  have desire, 27–29
  have a dream, 14–15, 21–24
  have faith, 29–30
  have fun, 24–27
  make their luck, 30–33
Super Bowl, 29
Supportive people, 24
  surrounding yourself with, 190
Symantec, 78, 145
Synergy, definition of, 168

Talent(s), 43–45
Task List, ACT!'s, 84
Tasks:
  assigning, 102
  focusing on important, 105
  identifying most important, 123
Teams, 8–9
  definition of, 168
  (*See also* Teamwork)
Teamwork, 168–172
Telephone:
  mobile, 1
  numbers, 80, 145
  scheduling calls, 120–121
Telephone tag, eliminating, 83
Tests, 5
Time:
  finding, 96
  lack of, 1
  prime, 113–115
  saving, 61
  value of, 92–95
  wasting, 96, 127
Time management, four techniques
  of, 123–128
Time-wasters, 127
Trial and error process, 33–34

Trust:
developing, 182
importance of maintaining, 178

Urgency:
creating, 102
importance as different than, 105
Utah Jazz, 9

Vacations, 132
Veeck, Bill, 26–27
Voice mail, 1

WAYMISH: Why Are You Making It
So Hard for me to give you my
money, 163
Weekends, 1
Wepner, Chuck, 31

WinFax PRO, 145
Winners, making people feel like,
183–185
Woods, Tiger, 10
WordPerfect, 51
Words and music, 130
Work:
doing the hardest first, 101
ethic, 5
hard, 30, 34
quality and timeliness of, 107
Work and play, 25–26
World War II, 23
World Wide Web, 146
Worry, 36
Writing, 104

Youth, 2